The Super Unofficial Atlanta Souvenir Guide

Kudzu Undercover

Setting a new standard
for responsible journalistic
investigations.

"If there's a coverup, we volunteer to conduct the strip search."

The Super Unofficial Atlanta Souvenir Guide

A Look at What Makes Atlanta Hot

A Kudzu Undercover Project

ENTHEA PRESS
Atlanta, Georgia

This book contains satire, parody, and colorful writing. It has been prepared solely in a spirit of fun. If you take offense at anything we have printed, you probably take life far too seriously. Instead of consulting a lawyer and threatening to sue us, we recommend seeing a good psychiatrist. He will help you understand that you were mistreated as a child and cannot help being such a thin-skinned malcontent. You will feel better and won't sue us. We will feel better, too.

We are an equal opportunity offender: we poke fun wherever it is warranted, regardless of race, sex, creed, or national origin. We are not looking to incite any grudge matches—unless, of course, it will bring all of us a lot of publicity.

THE KUDZU UNDERCOVER TEAM

Writing and photography — Carl Japikse
Cartoons and artwork — Nancy Maxwell
Research — Rose Japikse
Special liaison — Leslie Swanson

THE SUPER UNOFFICIAL ATLANTA SOUVENIR GUIDE

 Printed in the United States of America. Direct inquiries to: Enthea Press, P.O. Box 1387, Alpharetta, GA 30239-1387.

ISBN 0-89804-825-7

Table of Contents

Hey!

Hey!

Here in the South, this little word means a lot. It could be translated as "hello," but with proper inflection and intonation, it means much more.

"I'm glad to see you. What've you been doing? Everything going all right?"

Southerners are like that. They know how to conserve energy and cram all those ideas into one tiny word. It's not that they are noncommunicative. It's just that when the temperature hits 95° for three or four weeks in a row, you learn to conserve energy. You learn to say more with less.

Hey—thanks for reading this unofficial guide to Atlanta. We hope it will help you understand Atlanta a bit better than before, whether you live in Atlanta, plan to live in Atlanta, used to live in Atlanta, or are just visiting. Our purpose in publishing this guide is to celebrate the fun side of Atlanta—and to occasionally poke fun at the more somber side.

We want to tell you why Atlanta is Hotlanta, and not just on the thermometer.

In preparing this guide, we decided it would be impossible to be comprehensive. We believe we have at least mentioned every major attraction in the area, and a number in outlying areas. But there is no way we could review every restaurant, every nightclub, every art gallery, every antique emporium, or every cutesy gift shop in Atlanta. Such a book would balloon to hundreds of pages, probably thousands. It would resemble the Sears catalog—and we all know what happened to it.

Instead, we have highlighted the attractions and shops that have made a lasting impression on us. There may well be others that deserve being in the book. If they do, let us know, and we'll try to pick them up in the next edition. But we make no guarantees.

We also make no apologies. We call them as we see them. Since this is an unofficial guide, we do not feel constrained to bow down in obeisance to official sacred cows. If something is good for Atlanta and its image, we have given it all that it deserves. If something else is just a lot of hot air and pomposity, however, we have not hesitated to puncture a few balloons.

We have not done this in meanness. It's all in the name of fun.

We also have a confession to make. We are not Atlanta natives. We are transplants.

What's worse—we are Yankee transplants. But we love Atlanta every bit as much as if we had been born here, perhaps even more. After all, we went to the trouble to move here.

In this regard, it might be helpful to keep in mind that Atlanta was founded by transplants. (Every town or city is, after all.) Nevertheless, it may seem to border on audacity for transplants to publish a guide to Atlanta—and a semi-irreverent one at that.

But then again, we didn't come up with Whatizit. Or the idea to make VISA Atlanta's official credit card. Or suspend billboards in the ozone.

Nor have we solicited official sponsors at $40 million a crack. We're unofficial, through and through.

The one thing we will take credit for is our alternate mascot, Whogivesadamn. You can read the whole story of this mascot in the comic strip that graces the middle of the book.

We would like to ask you, dear reader, to lend your support for Whogivesadamn. It's a way of making your voice heard. Who knows? If he doesn't succeed in replacing Whatizit, he could at least be a viable candidate for president in 1996.

The nice thing is that you can show your support just by doing nothing. That is the essence of Whogivesadamn's message, after all. But if you are one of those activists who think they ought to be doing something, regardless of how stupid the cause, here are some ideas:

Buy our Whogivesadamn T-shirts.

Buy our Whogivesadamn license plate tags for the front of your car.

Buy our Whogivesadamn coffee mugs.

Buy anything and everything we can think up to merchandise this mascot.

It's a way to make your voice heard. And it's in the spirit of the Olympics, the Super Bowl, and everything that makes Atlanta great.

At the very least, buy this book. Purchase of it automatically confers on you status as an "unofficial sponsor" of every event hosted in Atlanta this year—plus the Olympics.

That's a lot more than even $40 million could buy.

Getting Around Atlanta

Who's driving the truck?

As unplanned as Atlanta is, it is relatively easy to learn your way around town—and the whole Metro area—once you accept a few basic principles:

• Almost no street runs straight. This is especially true as you get out toward and beyond the perimeter, where many of today's roads follow the pig trails of 100 years ago. Apparently the pig farmers were drunk or had little control of their herds, because these roads can and do wander all over creation.

• Nearly every road contains the name Peachtree in it somewhere, as in Peachtree-Dunwoody or Peachtree Industrial Boulevard.

• The few major roads other than Peachtree are either fords, ferries, or bridges, as in Shallowford Road, Paces Ferry Road, or Holcomb Bridge Road. These roads will eventually lead you to the Chattahoochee River.

• Because the Chattahoochee bisects metro Atlanta, there are only a few major connectors between Atlanta and the cities to its west and north. If you are going to Marietta or Dunwoody, you had better be on one of these connectors, or you will never get where you're going.

Metro Atlanta is divided into two sections—the part inside the perimeter (formed by Interstate 285 encircling the city) and the part outside. The part inside is likewise split in two. The western half is the city of Altanta. The eastern half is Dekalb County—primarily the city of Decatur.

Interstates 75 (from Chattanooga and Miami) and 85 (from Greenville and Montgomery) form a giant X that could almost be construed as a replica of the bars in the Confederate battle flag, except that everyone would be offended and it would be too expensive to tear up all that concrete. So just think of it as an X from a giant tic-tac-toe game, with the Perimeter forming the O. Interstate 20, from Birmingham to Augusta, intersects with the other two at their crosspoint, which is roughly Downtown. As a result, if beginning at Downtown, you can reach any point on the Perimeter in about 20 minutes, except at rush hour, when you should be taking a nap.

MARTA's rapid transit is a great way to get around

In Atlanta, the most important street is Peachtree, which runs north from Five Points. This road is so important that it actually splits into two parallel streets, East Peachtree and West Peachtree, that run parallel to each other for several miles at Midtown. This bidirectional ambiguity may help explain the nature of Midtown.

To complete the confusion, Peachtree begins as Peachtree Street, but changes to Peachtree Road above Midtown.

The reunited Peachtree continues all the way to Buckhead, where it veers to the northeast, to Brookhaven. Its northerly

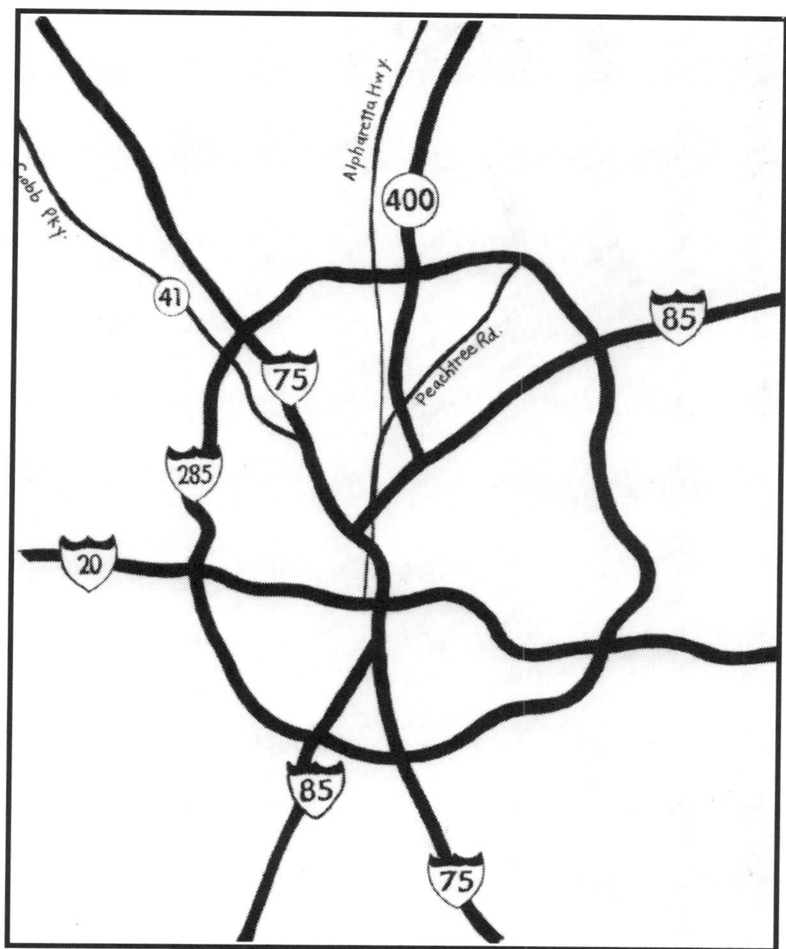

The Easiest Places To Get Mugged

A visitor from Los Angeles marvelled at how safe he felt walking around downtown Atlanta at night, and how clean and free of graffiti the city was. In spite of this endorsement, however, there are places where Atlanta may not be much safer than Los Angeles:

1. Any Atlanta high school.
2. Techwood.
3. Lakewood.
4. West End Mall.
5. Midtown.
6. Thomasville.
7. The MARTA at night.
8. The Fulton County Property Tax Assessment Board in the broad daylight.

course is picked up by Roswell Road, which can be taken all the way up to Dahlonega, if you care to.

The faster route to the northern suburbs, however, is to take I-85 north from Downtown, then exit to Georgia 400. A 50-cent toll must be paid at Buckhead, but from there on it is clear sailing all the way to the Perimeter (I-285), Dunwoody, Roswell, Alpharetta, and points north.

Almost every attraction, site, or restaurant seems to be located somewhere on or close to Peachtree Street/Road, so once you learn where it is, you can find 75 percent of everything in Atlanta worth finding. And a good map plus a sense of direction should be all that you need to find the rest of them.

If you prefer not to drive, there are many fine alternatives:

• MARTA, the metro area's excellent rapid transit system. You can reach most of the major attractions in Atlanta by MARTA and not have to worry about finding a parking place Downtown. It runs north-south from Doraville to the airport, and east-west from Hightower to Indian Creek. Tokens cost $1.25. Buses run to parts of the metro area that are not served by the train.

MARTA sign

• Guided tours are offered on a daily basis.

• The most romantic way to get around, at least Downtown, is by horse and buggy. Several firms offer buggy rides, operating guided tours starting from Underground and major downtown hotels. Prices range from $25 to $40. A champagne ride may be extra.

• The most cost-unconscious way to view Atlanta, of course, would be to charter a helicopter or small plane and view it from above.

• By far the cheapest way to tour Atlanta is on foot—the walking tour.

A Cluster of Cities

Atlanta is unique among large American cities in the way it has developed. In the typical big city, there is a large core in the official city, surrounded by an equally large population in suburbs that grew up around the central core as it evolved. The story of Atlanta is considerably different. With 395,000 residents, it is a relatively small city surrounded not by suburbs but by other towns that are cities in their own right:

Decatur (17,000.)
Marietta (44,000).
Smyrna (31,000).
Roswell (48,000).
Alpharetta (13,000).
Dunwoody (26,000).
Peachtree City (19,000).

Peachtree and Roswell roads in Buckhead

Many of these towns are older than Atlanta itself. Decatur was already established as the county seat of DeKalb County when the stake that became Atlanta was first driven. In fact, Atlanta was originally part of DeKalb County. When the new residents got tired of riding all the way to Decatur to conduct official business, they petitioned to secede from DeKalb County. Thus was Fulton County born.

Roswell was already a prosperous mill town by the time Atlanta began developing. And Marietta was the first stop on the Western & Atlantic railroad after it left Atlanta heading for Chattanooga.

As the Atlanta area grew, all of these cities grew as well, forming the huge Atlanta metropolitan area of more than 3 million people.

Atlanta itself, however, is doomed to remain relatively small. Growth is blocked in virtually every direction—by the Chattahoochee on the west and north and by DeKalb and Clayton counties to the east and south.

This pattern of growth is reflected in the fact that there are at least a half dozen "downtown" areas in the metro area—clusters of office buildings, stores, skyscrapers, and hotels that serve as centers of metropolitan activity. The five largest concentrations of activity of this kind are: Downtown, Midtown, Buckhead, the Cumberland complex at I-75 and I-285, and the intersection of I-285 and Georgia 400.

If all these areas were grouped together in a single district, as they are in most cities, it would be almost overwhelming. It is a tribute to Atlanta that it has diversified its "downtown" growth.

This diversification follows through in the residential character of the city as well. Atlanta is a city of small towns or neighborhoods which grew up independently but share the same government. Each of these neighborhoods has its own character and role that it plays:

Five Points is downtown.

Auburn Street has been the center of black achievement and culture.

Midtown is a second downtown complex, halfway between Five Points and Buckhead. It features Piedmont Park and the Botanical Gardens.

Buckhead boasts some of the most spectacular skyscrapers in the area, and is a center of exclusive shopping, excellent hotels, and fine dining. It is a wealthy community.

Virginia Highlands enjoys a high concentration of ethnic restaurants and off-beat shops.

Druid Hills is a wealthy residential community.

Sweet Auburn Street

Common Scents

In getting acquainted with Atlanta, don't forget your nose. One of the best ways to discover the real Atlanta is to sniff it out. The city abounds with thousands of odors and fragrances, most of them delightful.

Downtown Atlanta, of course, smells like most any large city. The common scent is automobile exhaust. As you move out from the congested city center, however, the nose begins to revive.

A butterfly garden in Roswell

Unlike most major cities, Atlanta has very little of the nose-clogging stench of heavy industry that blights so many American metropoli.

There are no stockyards as there are in Kansas City or Chicago. There are no paper mills, as there are in other Southern cities. There are no oil refineries, as there are in Philadelphia. As a result, it is possible to sit in quiet repose in the fragrance garden at the Atlanta Botanical Gardens and inhale the subtle fragrances of aromatic shrubs and flowers, just moments away from the rumble and noise of Piedmont Avenue.

Other great getaways that let you "smell the flowers" include Fernbank and the gardens at the Atlanta History Center.

Atlanta is a city where flowers of one sort or another are always in bloom, and many of the most wonderful fragrances come from trees and gardens:

- The honeysuckles and lilacs in the early spring.
- The dogwoods and crabapples heralding summer—and the need to mow the grass.
- The hibiscus and crepe myrtle in the heat of summer.
- The unequalled bloom of the magnolia.
- The subtle emanations of lilies.

These odors are one of the great treasures of Atlanta, and they are constantly on display, for the pleasure of the area's residents as well as tourists.

Some of the other notable scents of Atlanta are:

- Barbeque wafting from rib shacks.
- The wetness of the Chattahoochee as you float downstream on a raft.
- Hot dogs at a Brave's game in Fulton County stadium.
- Horse farms in Alpharetta.
- The habitats of Zoo Atlanta.
- Pine straw.
- Sweat at the finish line of the Peachtree Road Race.

If you really want to get to know Atlanta, follow your nose! Get out of your car and walk the streets of each neighborhood, sniffing out the best smells as well as the most picturesque sights. Fill your lungs with the essence of this city.

After all, there is nothing so uncommon as common scents.

Getting ready to grill brats at a Brave's game

Breakfast in Atlanta

Owing to our European heritage, many folks in this country do not pay much attention to the meal of breakfast. If they have time for a Danish and coffee on the fly, it is good enough for them. If push comes to shove, they may cut out breakfast altogether—and even feel smug about it.

Thank God for the South, which knows how to fix, serve, and eat a proper breakfast. And thank goodness it is possible to find a decent place to be served breakfast on just about every street corner in metro Atlanta.

We're not talking Egg McMuffins here, made of composition ham, artificial cheese, and pretend eggs. We're talking real food, Southern style:

Big ole biscuits, freshly baked and served piping hot.

Sausage gravy.

Bacon, sausage, or ham.

Grits or hash brown potatoes.

Two or three eggs.

Pancakes or waffles.

Ahhh.

Our favorite place for breakfast is the Waffle House, and not just because they are head-quartered here in Atlanta. These folks know what they are doing, and achieve a high level of consistency from one outlet to another—even though there are scores of them in Atlanta alone.

How many times have you been in a short-order establishment—and breakfast must be fixed and served to order—and asked for eggs, only to have the cook crack a couple of eggs on the hot stovetop and fry them to death? Or cook an omelet on the same stovetop, wrapping it up like a sheaf of scrambled eggs? At the Waffle House, they cook their eggs in individual pans. As a result, the omelets are fluffy and sunny-side up looks like something you would enjoy seeing in the morning.

Even poached eggs—the ultimate test of short order cooking—are prepared the way they ought to be.

The waffles which give them their name are also first rate, especially the pecan waffle.

And yes, each of these meals is served with grits. To Northerners, grits are one of the mysteries of the South. To Southerners, however, the only mystery is why Northerners don't eat grits, too.

Actually, many Northerners do—they just do not realize it. Polenta is basically the same thing as grits, but served with a different meal.

In the South, breakfast would be incomplete without grits. It is part of the Southern character, part of their constitution.

Some people suggest that you have to develop a taste for grits, in much the same way you have to develop a thirst for whisky. This is somewhat misleading. Grits grow on you. Every time you eat them, they become more and more a natural part of your breakfast fare. It's not an addiction; you could live without grits. But you're not sure you would want to. At this point, grits have become one of life's pleasures.

In addition to the Waffle House, there are many fine places to catch breakfast around Atlanta:

The Cracker Barrel, if you happen to be near either I-75 or I-85.

Hickory House, at various locations.

Dunk 'n Dine.

Le Peep, if you are looking for a California version of breakfast.

Applebee's, an Atlanta chain with many metro locations, serves some marvelous breakfast items as brunch on Saturdays and Sundays.

Or any hotel with a dining room.

Whatever your tastes, breakfast in Atlanta is just too promising to miss.

An Architectural Tour

As a city grows, it often develops an architectural style that distinguishes it from other towns and regions. Baltimore is known for its row houses; New Orleans for its stately mansions. Chicago can boast about its influence on early skyscrapers. But Atlanta has yet to develop a trademark of its own, architecturally.

This is not to say that Atlanta lacks style, beauty, or grace, however. It is a city of enormous beauty. But much of this beauty is derived from its natural assets, not manmade ones.

Think of the major American cities. New York, Washington, Houston, Los Angeles, and Chicago. Not a one of them can touch Atlanta in terms of natural beauty. Everywhere you turn in Atlanta, there are trees and gardens. Even on the interstate, just five minutes from downtown, it seems as though you are in the middle of the country.

In part, this is the legacy of cotton. One hundred years ago, Atlanta was the capital of the cotton-growing South. Almost every acre of arable land in the region was planted in cotton. There were no lush pine forests or gardens. Just cotton. But year after year of planting cotton soon killed the land; the cotton had drained the soil of the nutrients it needed to grow more cotton—or anything else.

The ruined land was worthless, and so it was abandoned back to nature. Mother Nature went to work. Where nothing else would grow, Eastern pines did. Whole forests grew up all over the region now referrred to as metro Atlanta. The pines eventually yielded to tulip trees and other specimens. As the rapid expansion outward from downtown occurred in this century, it gobbled up forested hills and dales—not farm land.

The State Capitol Downtown

The Georgian Terrace in Midtown

The "worthless" land ruined by cotton, incidentally, now brings as much as $50,000 an acre as far away as thirty miles from Five Points.

Two other factors have also been important in shaping modern Atlanta.

First, the town was virtually destroyed by the Civil War, so no antebellum architecture remains. The entire history of architectural tradition in Atlanta is therefore a scant 125 years old. Indeed, one of the first major projects in which architectural principle was truly important was the state capitol building, which was finished in 1890.

When Roswell King began building the town of Roswell in the 1830's, he imported a highly respected architect from Connecticut to design all of the major residences and municipal buildings. As a result, the town of Roswell actually has an

This Buckhead complex *straddles* GA 400

architectural tradition that is 40 years older than that of Atlanta!

Much of Atlanta's growth has occurred without this kind of coherent plan. It has grown in response to the boom town fever that has characterized Atlanta from the very beginning—first as a railroad boom town, then as the capital of cotton, next as the New South, and more recently as the heart of the modern South. There has been no real letup in the expansion of the metro area since the Civil War.

The city's architecture does illustrate this pattern of growth fairly well. It is fresh and youthful in many ways—it conveys the spirit of a brash, confident, upstart city that is going to prove its worth and vitality to the rest of the world, whether the rest of the world pays attention or not.

As you try to become familiar with metro Atlanta architecturally, look for these elements of exuberance, dignity, and freshness. You can find them in the major clusters of skyscrapers, but also in a few unsuspected places.

In evaluating the architecture of any city, there are five major categories to consider:

- Government buildings.
- Gathering places, such as a stadium.
- Churches.
- Business and commercial buildings.
- Private residences.

Of all the government buildings, the only one with any interest is the Capitol, which is a good example of the classical revival style. Most of the other state buildings are boring boxes that could just as easily be located in Pittsburgh or Chicago as here. To make matters worse, the lovely capitol building is surrounded by these sterile boxes. Instead of dominating the skyline, it is actually dwarfed and hidden. Even the striking gold dome (covered with gold leaf from Dahlonega) is hard to see from many angles.

Public gathering places do little to help the shape of Atlanta, either. Fulton County stadium is attractive but not stunning. The Omni looks like a large nest for gigantic insects. The World Congress Center is a little bit more interesting than the average warehouse—and the Georgia Dome is far more impressive on the inside than on the outside.

The one intriguing note among public gathering places are a number of the MARTA stations, which were designed with some measure of style, imagination, and grace. Even if you do not use MARTA to go anywhere, you should at least ride it to see some of the graceful stations.

The churches of Atlanta are scattered throughout the city; most of them reflect the trends current at the time they were built. There are some impressive structures, but in most cases the churches were content to serve Atlanta spiritually,

DuPont's offices in Central Park

The Concourse at I-285 and Georgia 400

not architecturally. There is one magnificent stretch of churches along Peachtree Road in Buckhead, just before it splits off at Roswell Road, as well as another one on East Ponce de Leon in Druid Hills, but their impact derives mostly from the cumulative effect.

The themes of confidence and exuberance are best expressed in the commercial and business buildings. The cluster of skyscrapers around Buckhead is especially interesting, specifically in the way it has solved the problem of blending modern freeway systems with rapid transit, shopping malls, and offices. Each of these can be a problem of modern design; in Buckhead, they have been combined harmoniously to create a stunning solution.

Another area where metro Atlanta excels is in office parks. In many cities, industrial parks are simply convenient ways to group a lot of eyesores together. In Atlanta, many of these complexes have been designed to be a great deal more beautiful and relaxing than most recreational areas. The Concourse and Central Park, both near the intersection of Georgia 400 and the Perimeter, are outstanding achievements of the very best in modern freeway office architecture. The Windward complex, further up 400, takes the park-like setting to an even higher level of achievement.

There were bold plans to bring some of these elements to Midtown and Downtown, but the economic slowdown has derailed many of them. Nor should Atlanta overlook the many areas of the city, primarily to the south and west, which were rapidly developed and then abandoned as commercial and industrial needs shifted.

As stunning as some of the business complexes are, however, the real focus of any architectural tour should be in the residential areas. Being a nonstop boom town, Atlanta has generated enormous wealth over the last 130 years. Much of this has been invested in building private residences, first in Buckhead and then elsewhere.

A great diversity of style and opulence can be discovered just by driving through Atlanta's neighorhoods. Some suggestions of where to cruise would include:

- West Paces Ferry Road, from Peachtree all the way to the Chattahoochee.
- Northside Drive from I-75 to I-285.
- Spaulding Drive through Dunwoody.
- Club Drive north of Peachtree in Buckhead.
- East Ponce de Leon through Druid Hills.
- The Prado section of Midtown.

Of course, some of the finest residences, from the Governor's mansion to the Swan House and the Herndon Home, are open for public touring.

Atlanta is filled with these architectural treasures.

Primrose Cottage on Mimosa St. in Roswell

Pitchtree, Georgia

It's a natural assumption to make. Everywhere you turn in Atlanta, it is Peachtree this and Peachtree that. There's even a magazine of style and fashion named *Peachtree*. The name is so common it is easy to start thinking, "There must have been a big ole peach tree, and they named everything—except the city—after it." After all, the peach is the official fruit of Georgia.

In actual fact, there was a Cherokee village along the banks of the Chattahoochee called Standing Peachtree. It is believed that Atlanta's main street, and just about everything else, has carried on this name. And the honor of peaches everywhere.

There is just one problem. Peach trees grow in southern Georgia, but they are not native to Atlanta. There never was a peachtree, in Standing Peachtree or in infant Atlanta.

It was a pitch tree.

A pitch tree? That's right—a tree that yields pitch, a tarry resin that was widely used to caulk ships. The subtropical pine forests of Georgia were famous for the pitch they produced. An especially large pitch tree could easily become a noted landmark—and did.

But not a very good landmark, for the process of obtaining the pitch eventually kills the tree, after a few years, and all you have left is lumber. By the time Atlanta was founded, the tree was the stuff legends are made of—sawdust—but its aura remained. It became the most common name in the new city.

As for Atlanta, it was originally called Terminus, a Latin word which roughly means "end of the line." This name was written on a stake hammered into the ground by a railroad surveyor who laid out the route for the new Western and Atlantic railroad, which was to run from Chattanooga to a yet to be determined spot in northwestern Georgia. The surveyor chose a spot just east of the Chattahoochee River—a spot that was chosen primarily to make it as easy as possible for a bridge to cross the river. He then followed a ridge eastward from the river several miles and drove his famous stake—perhaps from lumber cut from Standing Peachtree.

Driven in 1837, the stake determined the eastern end of the new rail line. It would be another 13 years before the line would be completed all the way to Chattanooga. In the meantime, lines were also completed to Augusta and Macon. Terminus was well on the way to becoming a railroad hub.

Terminus prevailed as a name only because no one actually lived at Standing Peachtree. As work began on the railroad, however, people quickly moved into the area. The early settlers decided to call their town "Marthasville," in honor of the daughter of a former governor of Georgia.

Once the railroad station was officially opened, however, the clerks found it cumbersome to write "Marthasville" on every voucher. They appealed to their boss, a transplant Yankee named J. Edgar Thompson. He saw the hardship of their plight and renamed the depot "Atlanta," since it was the Atlantic end of the Western and Atlantic railroad. Soon, no one was talking about going to Marthasville anymore. Everybody who was anybody was going to—or coming from—Atlanta. Eventually, the town fathers surrendered and changed names once more—to Atlanta.

We think of Atlanta as a gateway to the West, but in conception it was the West's gateway to the East—to the Atlantic.

And what does Atlanta have to do with peaches, anyway? Absolutely nothing. The word "Atlantic" means the sea of Atlas, the mythological figure who holds the world on his shoulder. Perhaps this sets a mythological tone for the future of Atlanta as a hub for the world; only time will tell.

Would the Olympic committee have chosen a city called Pitchtree, Georgia, to be the site of the 1996 Games? Not likely. But Atlanta—this is a name with strength and vitality. Which makes us glad Atlas didn't have a daughter named Martha.

Caught up in Kudzu

If you have spent any time at all in Atlanta, you know about kudzu. It is a creeping vine that is most commonly seen along the highways, draped like crepe paper over pine trees that it has killed. Kudzu climbs over stop signs, fences, old sheds; it invades gardens, roadways, and anything left untended during the summer growing season. It is almost universally cursed throughout the South as the worst parasite to invade the region since the carpetbaggers.

The kudzu leaf

What not everyone realizes, however, is that kudzu is not native to the South. It is not even native to the U.S. Kudzu comes from Japan, where it is highly regarded as a source of fiber for weaving baskets, a food (of course, they eat seaweed, too), and a secret ingredient in their various aphrodisiac powders.

A law of its own

How did kudzu arrive in Georgia? Was it part of an evil Japanese plot in World War II to conquer America by choking us to death as we lay sleeping at night?

It was imported, deliberately, by a Southern farmer who thought it might be a good way to stop soil erosion. He planted it on his farm, but no one knows how the experiment turned out. The farmer disappeared without a trace the next year. The kudzu was widely suspected as the culprit, but there was no proof. Investigators went to study his farm, but they were never able to locate it. All they found was acre after acre of kudzu.

Kudzu is named after the Japanese town of Kuzu, which is said to produce the finest quality of kudzu in the world. This must rank at the top of history's greatest dubious achievements.

The problem of kudzu in the South is that it has no natural enemies. In Japan, there are various insects that nibble on it, thereby keeping it in check. In the South, we are up to our ears in bugs and pests, but not one of them eats kudzu. As a result, kudzu grows and grows, not in the deep forests, but in clearings. And as it grows, it strangles its host.

Not long ago, a child in Atlanta wandered off from his family and was missing for days. A massive search was conducted, but he remained lost. He was finally found a short distance from his home—under a patch of kudzu.

It looks as if kudzu is here to stay, so we had better learn to make money on it somehow. Turn it into a cash crop. Perhaps Ted and Jane will promote it as the ideal side dish to buffalo. Or bribe a bunch of researchers to claim that eating kudzu is even healthier than oat bran.

Ghost forest: kudzu strangles giant pines into submission

If that does not work, Atlanta should hold an International Kudzu Festival in the year 2000, offering prizes for the best idea for commercial exploitation of kudzu.

By the year 2001, the lost city of Atlanta would have entered history as a mystery greater than the Bermuda Triangle:

Gone with the kudzu.

Chop Until You Drop

Fans pour into Atlanta's Fulton County stadium

Eighty-one times a year—more if all goes well—almost 50,000 Atlantans endure traffic jams, parking lot nightmares, and packed MARTA trains to converge on Fulton County stadium. Are they drawn by a political leader? No way. Are they attending a religious ritual? Some might say so, but it is not true.

They are attending a home game of the Atlanta Braves, the local entry in the National League West—and having the time of their lives. Few forms of mass entertainment have endured quite so well as major league baseball, now well into its second century of competition. Thirty years ago, gloomy pundits were predicting that baseball was a dying sport—that fan interest was shifting to football. In 1993, the Braves drew 3.9 million fans to watch its regular season home games, an all-time record.

Fred McGriff takes a cut at a breaking ball

It hasn't always been this rosy, of course. Just a few years ago, owner Ted Turner had to stoop to pig races and other silliness to draw people out to the ball park. And Atlanta is actually the third home of the Braves, who started playing ball more than 100 years ago in Boston. They moved to Milwaukee in the early 1950's, unable to compete with the Red Sox. Fifteen years later, fan support in Milwaukee had chilled as well, despite Warren Spahn, Lew Burdette, and the incomparable Hank Aaron, and the franchise moved south, becoming the first major league team below the Mason-Dixon Line.

There is one reason why the fans fill up the stadium for each home game now—the Braves are winning. They have won back to back National League pennants in 1991 and 1992, and came within a whisker of repeating it in 1993, only to

David Justice records an out in right

The Art of the Chop—Fans demonstrate their own individual styles of executing the Chop

lose to the unshorn Phillies in the playoffs. The regular season race for the division title was one of the greatest races ever, with both the Braves and the San Francisco Giants playing baseball as well as it can be played. The pennant was decided on the last day of the season, as the Braves won.

It is hard to imagine anything more entertaining than three hours at a Braves game. The Braves are not just an excellent team; when they are in their stride, it seems as though they can do whatever it takes to win a ball game. If the pitcher gets into trouble, they are able to get the other team to ground into a double play that ends the inning. If the Braves are down by two runs in the 7th or 8th inning, Ron Gant or David Justice or Fred McGriff will hit a home run that puts them back in the lead.

In addition, there is a rapport between the Braves and their fans which seldom exists at a professional level. The fans do not just cheer—they chop. This is an audio-visual display borrowed a couple of years ago from Florida State, executed by making a chopping motion with the hand while cheering, "Oooo-waaa-ooo"—just like Indian braves on the warpath, or so we suppose.

The Braves may well be one of the best teams in baseball history, if free agency does not decimate it after a few years. Oddly enough, they seem to play baseball as it was played in the glory days of the Teens and Twenties, instead of the high tech Nineties.

It can certainly be argued that Blauser to Lemke to McGriff may be one of the very best double play combos since Tinker to Evans to Chance first defined the importance of the double play. Jeff Blauser even looks like he should have been playing ball with the likes of Ty Cobb and Lou Gehrig.

And who can cast stones at the Braves pitching staff, which features three Cy Young winners and several more probable winners? Glavine, Maddux, Smoltz, and Avery are artists at their craft.

The Braves are easily the number one choice as hottest ticket in Atlanta. And, after managing the comeback of the century, it is a pity they did not make it to the World Series and a grudge match with Toronto. That would have been more than hot. It would have been scorching.

Steve Avery warms up under the watchful eyes of Leo Mazzone and the owl

A Delight at Every Turn

The rapid change in our society from a rural, agricultural nation to an urban, technical community has deprived many Americans of the opportunity to interact first-hand with nature—to see a bee sipping nectar from a clump of flowers or the brilliance of wildflowers waving in the hot summer breeze. This, in turn, has led to a loss of imagination—the fine knack for seeing not just bees flitting among the flowers, but also sprites and sylphs—or water nymphs bathing in the cascades of a miniature waterfall.

Pan plays his flute from a hiding spot

Atlanta is fortunate to have access to a wondrous place, right in the heart of Midtown, that brings back these opportunities. It is the Atlanta Botanical Gardens, and even though it has been in operation less than 20 years, it is one of the true treasures of Atlanta life.

The gardens are carved out of 60 acres of Piedmont Park, just five minutes from both I-75 and I-85. There are three main areas: the woodlands, the gardens, and the conservatory.

The woodlands are basically God's garden—an area of dense trees that has been left to grow, with only a minimum of help from the attentive hands of the botanical staff. A paved walkway has been cut through the forest, and even on the hottest day, a walk through the woodlands is cool and pleasant. Even though the business of the city continues to press forward just yards away, here in the woodlands it is possible to slow down, relax, and commune with life. A gentle brook wends its way through a magnificent collection of ferns, and sculpture and ponds are tucked away here and there, awaiting your discovery. And don't overlook the overlook, from which you can see the entire gardens, conservatory, and Atlanta skyline beyond.

The best section is the garden area. Winding walkways lead you from one kind of garden to the next—from the herb garden to the rose garden to the Japanese garden, and so on. Some of the gardens, like the rose garden, are the size of a ballpark; others, like the iris garden, are small enough to fit in an apartment terrace.

The staff has done

The Big Chicken?

A lily pond in front of the conservatory

A spectacular display of cacti

an impressive job with these gardens; as you walk along, it seems as if there is a new delight at every turn. A sculpture of a deer on loan from the High Museum looks out from behind a flowering bush; a sundial graces the center of the herb garden, reminding us all that the time we note on our watches and clocks is not really the Sun's time: it is a sloppy mixture of Atlanta's position in the time zone combined with human desire to get one more hour of daylight in the summer time.

Looking toward the Dorothy Chapman Fuqua Conservatory and the hazy Atlanta skyline beyond

One of the most striking gardens is the lily pond in front of the conservatory. The blooming lilies and lotuses on display in the pond are things of unparalleled beauty, images worthy of contemplating all afternoon.

The conservatory itself houses an impressive display of tropical and desert plants. Anytime you want to be reminded that Atlanta is not the hottest and most humid spot on earth, just come to the conservatory. It serves its purpose as a hothouse quite admirably, featuring giant ferns and exotic flowers, as well as a number of friendly birds who may, if you are lucky, put on an aerial exhibition.

A tremendous amount of love and labor has been invested in making the Atlanta Botanical Gardens the spectacular attraction that it is. When you come to visit, plan on spending several hours—or even the whole day. This is not a place to race through; the proper pace at which to enjoy its manifold charms is a sedate amble. Unless you are willing to sit as much as you walk (and many, many benches invite you to do so), it will not be possible to absorb the full measure of beauty and peace that embraces these gardens.

The Atlanta Botanical Gardens is located at Piedmont Park in Midtown. Admission is $4.50, half price for seniors and students. If you are a resident looking for civic activities to support, the Gardens deserve to be high up on your list.

It's the kind of thing that makes Atlanta great.

A Botanical Quiz—Which one of these nymphs cavorting in the Botanical Gardens is part of the permanent display? Rose in the entrance to the Japanese garden? Or the girl with the parasol in the Iris garden? For the answer, you will have to visit the gardens yourself.

The Tastes of Atlanta

Since the emergence of Hartsfield as an international air hub, the opportunities for dining out in Atlanta with a global flair have expanded rapidly. It is now a simple proposition to find a restaurant featuring any cuisine desired—Cuban, Spanish, Mexican, Thai, Vietnamese, Russian, Moroccan, Greek, or Korean—prepared with authentic ingredients flown in from the chef's native land.

Many of these restaurants are excellent and are, of course, a most welcome addition to the Atlantan scene. They complete the smorgasbörd of culinary traditions available here. But they do not *define* the tastes of Atlanta. For that, we must never forget that the South has its own noble culinary tradition: good ole Southern cookin'.

The most important thing that distinguishes Southern cooking from everything else is the importance of vegetables. In Atlanta, many restaurants offer a plate of four or five freshly cooked veggies as an entrée. In the rest of the country, you are lucky if a restaurant offers any vegetable at all; it is often replaced by a nondescript tossed salad.

The favorite vegetables of Southern cuisine, other than the now famous fried green tomatoes, run the gamut from sweet potatoes (yams), squash, green beans, and spinach to okra, black-eyed peas, and collard greens. Corn on the cob is frequently grilled, not boiled, and is excellent when prepared correctly.

One of my favorite places for vegetables is at Mick's, a local chain with many locations throughout the city. They grill carrots and broccoli and serve them hot from the charcoal. Their tomato soup is also outstanding.

Next to vegetables, chicken is king here. It is truly amazing how many restaurants in Atlanta specialize in chicken. You can get it fried, rotisseried, fingered, grilled, baked, barbequed, pulled, pattied, and poached. Two local chains, Chick-fil-a and Mrs. Winners, offer it as fast food. Chicken Chalet will deliver a rotisserie chicken to your front door, if you are within their driving range.

No chicken meal would be complete, however, without cornbread, another staple of Southern cuisine. In fact, bread is a very important ingredient in all Southern cooking. The reputation of a restaurant can rise or fall with its biscuits. The sweet biscuits at L & N Seafood restaurant are exceptionally good, as are the hush puppies at Skipper Sam's in Roswell, another seafood place.

If your craving is more toward a steak, you can always find satisfaction at such high-end establishments as Bones or Chops in Buckhead. For something more moderate in price, try any of the many Longhorn Steak Houses around town. In addition to a whole line of beef steaks, they have a first-rate salmon steak. They are also one of the few places to serve baked sweet potatoes as a side order.

Reviews of selected restaurants are scattered here and there throughout this book. We have made no effort to make a definitive list of "the best"—many outstanding restaurants are not included. These are restaurants that tickled our fancy for one reason or another. They offer something unique.

If you are looking for a meal to remember, you will not be disappointed.

Where To Shop

Shopping in Atlanta has changed a great deal since 1867, when Hungarian-born Morris Reich came from Chattanooga and opened a small dry goods shop on Whitehall Street. Starting with $500 capital loaned to him by his brother, Morris netted $5,000 in gross sales his first year. His first storefront disappeared a long time ago, but there are now Rich's stores "all about the South"—and in just about every mall in Atlanta.

Reich was not the only person to prosper by selling to Atlantans. Atlanta is a town where you can find virtually anything you might care to buy—and if you don't buy it, someone else will.

Actually, it's a fun place to shop. It has its malls, of course, and they do tend to dominate the shopping scene. But there is more to shopping in Atlanta than just going to Sears, Penneys, Macy's, and Rich's. There is variety. There are bargains. There can even be excitement.

The food court at Lenox Mall

If you have a lot of money, the place to head is Buckhead. At Lenox Mall, you will find the only Neiman-Marcus in the area, along with boutiques for designers Laura Ashley, Alexander Julian, and Ralph Lauren. If that is not enough, across the street is the newly rejuvenated Phipps Plaza, featuring The Parisian, Saks Fifth Avenue, Lord and Taylor, Tiffany & Co., Gucci, Abercombie & Fitch, Lillie Rubin, and others.

Scattered along Peachtree and Piedmont are scores of other stores, selling everything from coffee beans to sterling silver, and just about everything in between.

If you want a new riding blanket for your horse, however, you'll have a hard time finding it in Buckhead. You'll probably have to travel up to Alpharetta and visit one of the innumerable tack shops associated with riding stables.

Residents of Atlanta, of course, would almost never think of going to Alpharetta to shop. To them, Alpharetta seems to be halfway to nowhere. But this prejudice soon may be ending, with the opening of North Point mall.

North Point is a collection of 172 stores, all assembled in a neat package just east of Georgia 400—at the Haynes Bridge Road. It includes a Rich's, Lord & Taylor, Sears, JCPenney, and Mervyn's, plus such exotic smaller stores as Cache, Bali Craft, Perfumania, Ozone Electronics (owned by Otis Nixon), The Gentle Jungle, and Maison du Popcorn. Two smaller shopping centers are being built adjacent to North Point, creating non-stop shopping from Haynes Bridge to Mansell.

Two other important malls in the Atlanta galaxy are The Perimeter, at the intersection of Georgia 400 and I-285 and Cumberland Mall, at I-285 and U.S. 41. The value of Cumberland Mall is enhanced by the presence across the street of the Galleria, a collection of boutiques attached to the Waverly Hotel.

Once you venture forth from the relative ease of shopping at a mall, it is important to know where to head. Downtown is still an important retail district, with many excellent shops. A logical place to begin is the newly resuscitated Underground, which features all kinds of specialty stores, many operating from pushcarts. Even though Rich's has closed its downtown flagship, there is still Macy's, Muses, and Brooks Brothers—and a collection of shops in the Peachtree Center Gallery.

If you are just starting to get your feet wet, it would probably be best to start Downtown and gradually work your way up Peachtree to Buckhead. As you pass through the various neighborhoods, you will encounter all kinds of shops. At Buckhead, you can either follow Peachtree to the right, and end up at the Lenox

Mall-Phipps Plaza complex, or you can continue your way up Roswell Road to Sandy Springs.

Shoppers who delight in getting high quality clothing at discount prices should get to know the Loehmann shopping centers.

For more bizarre tastes in shopping, try browsing through the shops in Virginia-Highlands or Little Five Points. Here you will find shops that appeal to people interested in alternate lifestyles.

Want something from Thailand or Korea, but cannot afford to travel to the Orient? Take a trip to northeast metro Atlanta instead. There is a heavy concentration of immigrants from many countries of the Far East living in DeKalb County. One stretch of Buford Highway in Doraville is especially famous for its Oriental shops.

Crabapple Corners

If you need some native American pottery or artwork to add to your collection, try some of the shops in Dahlonega. Even though the gold mines in Dahlonega are responsible for the forced evacuation of the Cherokees from northern Georgia, it is still very much in the center of Cherokee territory today.

One of the most popular forms of bartering in Atlanta is through flea markets, both transient and permanent. One of the established flea markets is the Kudzu Flea Market, located at 2874 E. Ponce de Leon Ave, in Decatur.

For those with a more selective taste in old things, an antique store can be found on almost every street corner of every commercial zone in the metro area. Some of the weightiest concentrations of antique stores are to be found in Buckhead, Roswell, Alpharetta, and Crabapple Corners. As a general rule, expect the prices to decrease as you go further from downtown—i.e., Crabapple Corners.

Don't overlook Hawthorne Village at 3032 N. Decatur Road in DeKalb County. It's a grouping of a dozen or so stores featuring collectibles and antiques.

If you have time on your hands and want to hit some factory outlets, there are a number of choices. There's a cluster of them around Helen, Georgia, in the northeast mountain region of the state. Helen is also known as "the Alpine Village" and is a very popular resort area. Calhoun, Georgia, halfway between Atlanta and Chattanooga on I-75, is also staking its claim to becoming a major focus of outlet stores.

Should your tastes (and pocketbook) run more

Jordan Sales and Salvage in Fayetteville is a bargain hunter's paradise

toward one-of-a-kind objets d' art, there are studios and galleries scattered throughout Atlanta displaying and marketing the finest in paintings, scuplture, and crafts, not just from the South but the entire world.

Condomart on Highland Avenue

The Frabel Gallery, with locations both in Buckhead and Downtown, exhibit the signed crystal sculptures of Hans Frabel. Greggie Fine Arts, at 6075 Roswell Road in Sandy Springs has an unusual collection of unframed paintings by old masters.

The Roswell Mill contains a number of studios as well as other intriguing shops; it is located at the intersection of Roswell Road (from Marietta to Roswell) and Atlanta Highway (which is also called Roswell Road as you get closer to Atlanta). On weekends in the summer, the Mill often features concerts from musical groups from the Sixties.

While in Roswell, be sure to check out the gallery of an artist's cooperative, The Arts Pavilion, at 1158 Canton Street. The studio features the fantasy paintings of Stan Bruns, sculpture, and crafts.

Two areas chock full of cute little shops are the Village of Stone Mountain and the town square of Marietta. These stores are guaranteed to overwhelm your good intentions not to give in to impulse buying!

The Best Place in Atlanta To Buy...

1. Photo supplies—Wolf Camera Co.
2. Videos—Dunwoody Versatile Video.
3. Condoms—the Condom Art Museum.
4. Ready-to-cook meals—Harry's in a Hurry.
5. Golf clubs—West Georgia Golf Company in Tallapoosa, Georgia.
6. Lingerie—Victoria's Secret.
7. Furniture—Haverty's.
8. Carpet—Dalton, Georgia is wall to wall with carpet discount stores, with delivery to Atlanta.
9. Old junk—the Kudzu Flea Market.
10. Lawn and garden stuff—Hastings.
11. Gifts—The Sophisticated Swine.
12. Books—Oxford Bookstore.
13. Rare books—Books & Cases.
14. Perfume—Perfumania in North Point.
15. Costumes and risqué gifts—Eddy's Trick Shop.
16. Cowboy boots—Morgan Boots on Cobb Parkway in Marietta.
17. Camping gear—High Country.
18. Coca-Cola memorabilia—The World of Coke.
19. Hardware—Home Depot.
20. Baked goods—Great Harvest Bread Co. in Roswell.
21. Shoes—Alpharetta Bargain Store.
22. Maps and atlases—Latitudes in Perimeter Mall.
23. Cakes—Mrs. Rhodes' Bakery.
24. Llamas and pot-bellied pigs—Llamas of Atlanta.
25. Birdseed—Chattahoochee Nature Center.
26. Bonsai plants—The Abbey of the Holy Spirit in Conyers.
27. A Pepsi—Forget it.

All Hail Zeus

On July 20, 1996, the Olympic Flame will be lit in Atlanta, signaling the beginning of three weeks of international pageantry and athletic competition—the 100th anniversary of the modern Olympic Games.

The choice of Atlanta was not a whimsical one. Years were invested in careful planning and preparation before Atlanta was chosen over Athens, Greece, by the International Olympic Committee in 1990.

Until now, most of this planning and preparation has been behind the scenes. Slowly, however, the tangible evidence of it is beginning to emerge. Television rights have been sold. Construction has begun on the Olympic Stadium, which will become the new home of the Braves once the Games are concluded.

Zeus hurling lightning

To the general public, the biggest sign of the coming Olympics has been the aggressive campaign to sell tee shirts, umbrellas, and other paraphernalia bearing the 1996 Olympics logo. Sales of these items have generated revenue for the games, but have also left some Atlantans wondering if substance will follow the hype.

Not everyone is pleased by the coming Olympics, of course. There are those who are afraid that their personal needs will be overlooked as Atlanta shifts its focus to the international scene. What they are forgetting is that neither the city nor the county is organizing the Olympics. No tax money is being diverted to fund it; no government officials are being siphoned away from other duties to make sure the Olympics works. The funding and planning is the responsibility of a corporation founded expressly for this one purpose—the Atlanta Committee for the Olympics Games (ACOG).

It is the nature of these Games that we will not really know how well ACOG is doing until July 1996 actually arrives. By then, of course, it will be too late for criticism—too late to change course. Appreciating this basic fact, ACOG has gone to some lengths to open itself up to input from all kinds of advisory groups, soliciting ideas from the local communities that will be affected by the Olympics programs.

Atlanta's logo

It is a tribute to Atlanta and its organizers that the city was chosen for these games. In one key way, Athens was by far the sentimental choice: it had been the host for the very first Olympiad in the modern era, in 1896. Those Games were held under the auspices of the King of Greece and inaugurated the Games as we now know them.

The idea for reviving the Olympics was the passion of the French Baron Pierre de Coubertin, who was not himself an athlete, but was a brilliant scholar. He was deeply impressed by the record of the original Olympiad and saw the value of resuscitating it—on an international scale.

The original Olympic Games were begun in 776 B.C. and were held every four years until 393 A.D.—a span of more than 1,000 years. Each Greek city-state—such as Athens, Sparta, and so on—sent athletes to compete in this festival. The winners of the competition became national heroes, much as they do today.

Even when city-states were at war with one another when the time of an Olympiad arose, they broke off their warfare and attended the competition. This was because the Olympiad in ancient times was first and foremost a religious ceremony, and only secondarily an athletic festival. To fail to attend the Olympics would be a tremendous insult to Zeus, leading to certain doom for the offending city-state.

The ancient Olympics were always held at the same location, Olympia, at the foot of Mount Olympus in western Pelepponesia. In Greek mythology, Mt. Olympus is the home of the gods in general and Zeus in particular. An elaborate complex, dominated by a temple to Zeus, was built in Olympia for the Games. The stadium where the athletic competitions occurred was erected nearby.

The original Olympics were dropped when Greece came under the occupation of Rome. In reviving the Games 1500 years later, the Baron hoped to promote the ideal of amateur athleticism against the increasing presence of professionalism. But without the religious dimension that dominated the ancient Games, the effort to serve the ideal of amateurism has been greatly diluted.

Mt. Olympus

The charter of the International Olympics Committee refers to the ideals of brotherhood, unity, and peace—that the Games are not just an athletic competition but an opportunity for people of all nations to come together and recognize that there are larger forces that bind them together.

These ideals may well be stronger and more important than the Baron's original goal of promoting amateurism.

Interestingly, Atlanta has an opportunity to put some of these greater dimensions back into the Olympics. One of the principal venues for many of the events will be Stone Mountain State Park. Stone Mountain is one of the most impressive stone outcroppings in the world—and will certainly be a dramatic, inspiring backdrop for the Games. Combined with the beauty of the metro area, it is almost as if Atlanta provides a natural stage for games of this type—a more than suitable Olympia for 1996.

Beyond the purely physical aspects of Atlanta, however, there is another, intangible factor that may make these Games stand out among the rest. Atlanta has proven itself to be a gathering point for the South and for the nation; now it has a chance to demonstrate its hospitality as a gathering point for the world.

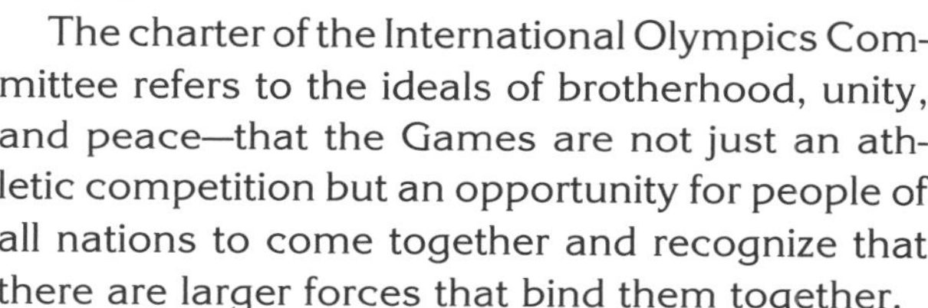

ACOG sketch of Atlanta's new Olympic stadium.

This is a factor that cannot be planned by any committee, of course. It must come from the hearts and minds of the three million people who call themselves Atlantans. The 1996 Olympics will put Atlanta on display—it is estimated that six out of every ten people on the planet will see at least some of the Games by television. ACOG is making sure that what the world sees will be physically impressive and serve the needs of the Games.

It is up to the people of Atlanta to make sure that the rest of the message is just as inspiring. The 1996 Games represent Atlanta's chance to extend the ideals of unity, peace, and brotherhood to the rest of the world.

The Thrill of the Rails

When all is said and done, Atlanta is a company town—an extraordinarily successful one, to be sure, but a company town nonetheless. The company: the railroads that literally put Atlanta on the map. The railroads still thrive in Atlanta hauling freight, but the glory days of thousands of people riding through Atlanta every day on endless lines of Pullman cars are long gone. Amtrak still passes through, picking up lonely souls that can't abide flying, but it is not the same.

Milepost Zero

For those who have never ridden the rails—or those who crave to ride a passenger train once more—there is a solution. The New Georgia Railroad offers the thrill of the rails in a short trip that usually lasts just three hours, and brings you back to your car!

Every Friday and Saturday evening, the train departs punctually from Milepost Station, right next to the Underground and the downtown Five Points MARTA station. As it chugs its way eastward, a full-course meal is expertly served.

Each of the railroad cars has been stripped down and completely refurbished, with elegant wood trimming, etched glass, and handsome serving areas. In keeping with the surroundings, guests are asked to dress appropriately: coat and tie for gentlemen, the equivalent for ladies.

The dinner is the main excuse for this excursion, of course, and it lives up to its billing. For us, it began with a superb cup of cream of Vidalia onion soup. The palate was refreshed with a small salad of leaf lettuce. A loaf of piping hot bread accompanied the salad.

There are usually three choices for dinner—beef medallions with bearnaise sauce, chicken, or fish. The latter two items vary with each trip. The beef was prepared quite well, and the bearnaise was excellent. The meat was served with redskin potatoes and a vegetable medley. Every bite was enjoyable.

Dinner dishes were whisked away while we stopped briefly at our eastern destination, the village of Stone Mountain. As we returned to Atlanta by twilight, we were served a choice of three desserts: a first-rate key lime pie, an excellent turtle pie, and carrot cake (the only one we didn't sample).

One of the cars has been converted into the kitchen, which resembles a stainless steel closet more than a working kitchen. But they bring forth excellent food—for 300 to 400 people—every night they make the run.

Highest marks of all go to the exceptionally fine service, which is constantly attentive but never obstrusive.

Alcoholic beverages are not sold on the train, but the servers will provide setups for those who choose to bring their own bottles. Champagne buckets were in prominent evidence, as this is a favorite way for many Atlantans to celebrate anniversaries.

Tickets to ride cost $39.50 a person and cover everything but a tip. Reservations must be made a week in advance; call 656-0769. The New Georgia also offers catered train service to Athens for University of Georgia football games and weekend excursions to Savannah and elsewhere.

Sherman Revisits Atlanta

General William T. Sherman was invited to attend the International States Cotton Exhibition—also known as the World's Fair—in Atlanta in 1881 to help celebrate Mexican Veteran's Day. Contrary to today's perception of Sherman as the evil genius who torched Atlanta, the reception given him just 16 years after the fact was extremely friendly.

Sherman took in the whole exposition, trading remarks with other soldiers about what battle was fought where, and so on. He had insisted ahead of time that he would not speak, but when he was introduced to the crowd, the response was overwhelmingly favorable, and cries went up for the general to speak.

Finally, he relented, and made the following remarks off the cuff:

"I have come today to look upon these buildings where once we had battlefields, and I delight more to look upon them than to look upon the scene which was here enacted sixteen years ago; and I say that every noble man and every kindly woman over this broad land takes as much interest in your prosperity and in this exposition as do those who are sitting in this presence today....

"As far as I am concerned, I am just as friendly to Georgia as I am to my own native state of Ohio."

Sherman's comments were greeted with "immense applause," as it is described in the report of the Atlanta *Constitution* reproduced below:

THE ATLANTA CO

VOLUME XIV. WEDNESDAY MORNING, NOVE

AT THE EXPOSITION.

FACTS AND INCIDENTS OF THE DAY NOTED.

The Largest Crowd Yet in Attendance The Gate Receipts Double those of Any Previous Day—Meeting of the Mexican War Veterans, and other Interesting Incidents.

The crowd of yesterday, which is noted more at length in the news matter below, showed conclusively that the exposition has reached a degree of success which must drive away every fear of failure in any respect whatever. Every day now is a day of successes and every week is better than its predecessor. The receipts are now nearly, if not quite, $15,000 a week, while the expenses are less than $3,000. This gives a margin that looks very much like the subscribers to the fund will be returned much of their money, and the exposition will be guilty of a thing unheard of before—paying back a very large per cent of the subscriptions.

Mexican Veterans' Day.

A LARGE ATTENDANCE AND MUCH ENTHUSIASM—THE ADDRESSES, ETC.

Yesterday was Mexican veterans' day, and the association held its meeting in Judges' hall at the exposition grounds. The crowd was the largest that has been on the grounds since the opening of the exposition. At three o'clock Judges' hall was filled with an eager audience to hear the address by General Jackson. Director-General Kimball conducted General Walker, General Jackson, and other distinguished men to the stage. General Sherman insisted on remaining in the audience.

When the applause which followed the appearance of the orator had subsided and the distinguished gentleman on the stage had been seated, Director-General Kimball arose and said:

Ladies and Gentlemen: This is the occasion of the annual meeting of the Mexican veterans and they have done us the honor to call their meeting here. It is their meeting and they will manage it in their own way. I have the honor to introduce to you General Walker.

General Walker, of this city, then arose and said:

At the close of the address General Sherman was loudly called for, and after a long hesitation he arose, and on being conducted from the audience to the stage, said:

Ladies and Gentlemen: I have told many to-day in Atlanta that my purpose was not to speak one word on this occasion. I came here to observe what you are doing here, of which I had read in the papers and been told about by other, who had seen the fair. But being here and being urged to speak a few words as an old Mexican veteran, I feel that I can refuse nothing to the soldiers, however averse I may feel toward doing so. I regard soldiery as being something so pure and ennobling that whoever has felt the spirit once can never forget it, and whenever I am called upon, whether it be by the soldiers of the Florida war or any other war, my heart responds as by inspiration. I see a few of my old comrades of the Mexican war here.

General Sherman then spoke of his connection with he Mexican war, in which he served with the cavalry. He then continued:

Now, gentlemen, we have heard the eloquent address of this memorable day. Its spirit is good, and I see no reason why we may not now declare with Webster: "Thank God, I am an American citizen." We are American citizens. I thank God that I am one, and I tell you that I can go to any spot from Maine to Texas, and stop where I please, so long as I behave myself and obey the laws of the place, and that is the spirit of the government. That is what made us the United States of America, and that is the foundation-stone upon which governments are built for this continent. We fought our mother and acquired our independence, and to-day we are the same nation, the same soldiers, the same government, the same flag, and, so far as I am concerned, I am just as friendly to Georgia as I am to my own native state of Ohio. [Immense applause.] If you all think Georgia is a better part of the country, why stick to Georgia, and if you want to go to California, why go there. That is the great value of our system of government. It is a government worth fighting for. I have come to-day to look upon these buildings where once we had battle-fields, and I delight more to look upon them than to look upon the scene which was here enacted sixteen years ago, and I say that every noble man and every kindly woman over this broad land takes as much interest in your prosperity and in this exposition as do those who are sitting in this presence to-day. I did not intend to be brought out even this much, but I think that we are all now in a position to say, every one of us, that we thank God that we are, each and every one of us, great and small, young and old, American citizens.

At the close of the address the large audience, after great cheering, rapidly dispersed, and thus ended the ceremonies of Mexican veterans' day at Judges hall.

The Crowd on Yesterday.

THE LARGEST BY ALL ODDS OF ANY DAY YET.

Yesterday showed the largest crowd that has governor's day. It is said that the gate receipts were more than double that of any other day, and as a consequence everybody was happy. The day was an unusually bright and pleasant one, and up to 4 o'clock crowds flocked through the gates. The excursion system has proved a grand success. The trains on all the roads came in crowded on yesterday. The Kingston excursion on the State road was simply overwhelmed with people. After selling 1,600 tickets, the agents at the stations refused to sell any more, as the train was already crowded to the utmost capacity. When it reached Atlanta, there was not standing room on the platforms of the cars. An excursion from the Central road, we believe from Americus and vicinity, came up loaded down the same way. It was estimated that these two excursions brought fully three thousand people, and as they arrived yesterday at about one o'clock, the bulk of them will not go out to the grounds until this morning, so that another big day may be expected.

In fact, there is no reason now to doubt that the attendance from now to the end of the exposition will be immense.

Visitors from Tennessee.

The city council of Nashville will not come to Atlanta to-day, but have postponed their visit for a couple of weeks. A special excursion rate is given from Nashville and quite a crowd is expected to-night. It is the time for the visit by the Tennessee press. The following members arrived last night: John E. Holmes, Morristown Gazette; D. B. Grace, Sweetwater Democrat; J. H. Bean, Knoxville Tribune; W. E. Brown, Rogersville Press and Times.

General Sherman's Visit.

General Sherman and his staff took rooms at the Kimball house upon reaching the city night before last.

On yesterday morning, in company with several gentlemen, they visited the grounds, and under the guidance of Senator Brown, Mr. Kimball, Secretary Ryckman and others, they made the tour of the buildings, which occupied them until about half past one. At that time they stopped at Mr. Kimball's office and rested for awhile. A number of ladies and gentlemen paid their respects to General Sherman for the succeeding hour. At half past two in company with Governor Brown, Mr. Kimball, Mr. Ryckman and others, the party visited Jones's restaurant and there had an elab-

It's All in the Drawl, Y'All

From the git go, it is easy to spot native Atlantans and separate them from the folks that have moved in from other parts of the country: Southerners speak with a drawl. The rest do not.

This is not an earthshaking revelation, of course. The Southern drawl is well documented—but not necessarily well understood. In fact, it is often portrayed comically in movies and television shows, as though it were a speech defect.

It is hardly that. If anything, it is a speech enhancement that should be studied, respected, and perhaps even imitated by people who have not grown up with it. The drawl is a pace of speech which actually allows people to think while they talk, instead of rushing to fill empty space with meaningless verbiage.

Here's a simple test you can make on your own. Spend five minutes listening to someone from New Jersey or Brooklyn talk nonstop. It will leave you feeling dizzy. Spend another five minutes listening to someone from California speak nonstop. It will leave you feeling dumb. Then spend five minutes listening to a true Southerner speak. It will leave you feeling relaxed, inspired—perhaps even poetic.

This is the way English was meant to be spoken. To the untrained ear, the Southern inflection—the drawl—may seem slow, lethargic. But the trained ear catches different rhythms. It hears the melodies of hummingbirds and bees flitting around honeysuckle on warm summer afternoons. It hears the cadences of James Dickey, William Faulkner, and the other poets and writers of the South. It hears the accumulated treasures of generation upon generation of storytelling, passed from parent to child.

It is no accident that the art of storytelling is preserved primarily in the South. In storytelling, the only instrument you have is your voice. If the sharps and flats, the dips and surges have all been flattened so that they sound like a dull twang, even the most fascinating story will end up putting everyone to sleep.

Southern speech has color, vigor, and life. There are actually two branches of Southern: white Southern and black Southern. The black branch is like a spoken version of gospel songs; white Southern is the carefully distilled blend of one part white lightnin' and one part Southern Comfort.

One of the best ways to get to know Atlanta, therefore, is by ear: to listen to the way the people you meet talk and communicate. Keep in mind that many people who live and work in Atlanta are transplants—they are not native Southerners. Also keep in mind that some Southerners conceal their drawl quite expertly, except when they are among their own. With them, you will have to listen for the disguised drawl behind the outer mask.

As you listen, here are some common Southern phrases and expressions to be alert for:

Good ole—a term of familiarity, as in "good ole boy" or "good ole truck."

Big ole—a term of comparison tinged with awe, as in "Thet big ole snow last winter trapped us indoors for a whole week."

Fixin' to—a term of anticipation or planning, as in "I'm fixin' to do thet right now."

Obliged—thank you.

Much obliged—thank you very much.

Evening—afternoon.

Good evening—good afternoon.

Do go on—you must be joking.

Church ain't out till the fat lady sings—the full version of an often misquoted phrase.

Go back on your raisin'—to pretend to be someone you aren't.

Happy as a dead pig in the sunshine—Could be the operative motto for Whogivesadamn.

Hard-down good—excellent.

I do declare—meaningless statement that is uttered when you can't think of anything to say.

It takes a big woman to weigh a ton—I suspect you are exaggerating.

Rip your drawers—make a mistake.

Useless as tits on a bull—of no value whatsoever.

Well, shut my mouth!—I have nothing to say.

These are colorful gems of human speech which enliven daily conversation, making it sparkle. In a day when television is homogenizing not only speech but thought, it is important to keep alive the color and texture of spoken Southern, drawl and all. It is one of the great contributions of the South to the rest of the nation.

So pick up your ears and pay attention, y'all.

Mr. John B's

One hundred years ago, John Broadwell was a prosperous cotton farmer in Alpharetta. An inventive fellow, he found a way of increasing the yield per acre of cotton by getting more cotton balls per plant. He called his hybrid "double jointed" cotton, and in 1911 he was honored by the governor of Georgia in a special ceremony. Samples of his cotton were put on display in the state capitol museum.

In John's time, cotton was king throughout the South. Atlanta had received international attention by holding the Cotton States Exposition in 1881. Most of the land in Alpharetta and Roswell was dedicated to the cultivation of the cotton plant.

John Broadwell was almost a crusader, travelling the area farms to preach the benefits of his innovative approaches to raising cotton. But he remained a man of the soil. His house, which survives, is a cozy but modest homestead, nothing like the grand plantations we associate with cotton growing.

The house was moved from its original location to Crabapple Corners a few years ago, and is now one of the most charming restaurants in the whole area, fittingly named "Mr. John B's."

This restaurant has it all—ambience, hospitality, and excellent food. It is open for lunch Monday through Saturday and for dinner Wednesday through Saturday.

When it first opened, the menu was pretty much Southern with a capital S. More recently, however, they have expanded into more exotic culinary fields, adding such decidedly non-Southern entrées as teriyaki tuna and chicken Marsala to the more traditional catfish platter and Maryland crab cakes.

Everything we have had at Mr. John B's has been excellent. A couple of favorites—Hardscrabble Beef and Country Captain—are not on the new menu, but the pork chop in Calvados and the crab cakes are, and they have always been first-rate. Dinners are served with a salad; lunches are served with soup.

New items that have won us over include pork loin with raspberry sauce, coconut salmon, grilled ribeye on eggplant, and chicken breast with crab and hollandaise.

Lunch items range from a Cuban Reuben with roasted pork and a stir fry veggie melt on a croissant to catfish fingers with fries.

For dessert, the restaurant serves up a wickedly delightful chocolate bourbon cake, as well as other baked goods—strudel, cobbler, and more.

It is hard to imagine a more charming dining experience than to sit in the living room of John B's home, a fire spitting in the hearth, indulging in the good food the restaurant serves. It evokes the spirit of a time gone by in a way that no museum or display can. Authentic tables and decor—Crabapple Corners is the heart of antique shopping in this area—complete the illusion.

In fact, they have even gone so far as to plant cotton in the garden area out front.

Mr. John B's is located at 780 Mayfield Road, 5 minutes west of the heart of Alpharetta. The telephone is 751-7381.

The John Broadwell Homestead in Crabapple

Porch Sitting

High-priced landscape designers are prone to talk about patios and decks as "outdoor living spaces," as though the idea of extending family life to the yard is a totally new concept. Folks in the South have been practicing this concept for years. It's called, "settin' a spell on the porch."

Porches developed as a necessity in those halcyon days before air conditioning. Whenever it became too hot to stay indoors, the family would migrate to the front porch and watch the world go by. If they were lucky, there would be a breeze to cool them down. If not, they made their own breeze with fans.

Porch sitting is a cultural tradition in the South. Almost every decent—and a good number of indecent—homes are built with a porch. The larger and grander the porch, the more affluent the family.

Of course, you cannot sit on a porch without furniture. The most common piece of porch furniture in the south is the rocking chair; even a front porch on a grand home like Bulloch Hall in Roswell is simply adorned with a string of basic rocking chairs. The rocking chair is the number one choice for porch sitting because the rocking movement of the chair helps stir up the air.

Many families, however, do not stop there. They will also install a couch, a cupboard or two, and perhaps some shelves. On hot summer evenings, they may bring a portable TV out and watch it on the porch.

Of course, this habit—like any habit—can be taken to extremes. Some people just do not know when to quit. Their porches end up looking like extensions of the broom closet instead of the living room. In some cases, the clutter spills over the porch and out onto the lawn. These are not your true picturesque Southern porches.

What does one do while porch sitting? As little as possible. It is all right to talk, of course, and it is assumed that teenagers on a date would find plenty to keep their interest. But the real purpose of porch sitting is to do next to nothing. The most industrious activities allowed on a porch are whittlin' and tobacco spittin'. If you want to read, go inside. Porch sittin' is a social activity.

It's part of the Southern way of living.

The Sophisticated Swine

The next time you need a gift, give yourself a treat as well—visit Sophie at the Sophisticated Swine. Sophie is a two-year-old pig who is one of three associates who conduct business at this nifty gift shop in a back alley of historic Roswell. Her two associates are humans, Ed Maddox and Don Daniels.

As youthful as she is, Sophie is carefully trained to help you pick out just the right item for any kind of gift giving. The shop carries all kinds of items, from humorous to eclectic, from inexpensive to pricey.

If you prefer to make your own selections, Sophie doubles as day care center. She will hold your children's attention the whole time you are browsing.

Our research department's Task Force on Cuteness has examined Miss Sophie and has declared her one of the Top Five cutest institutions in metro Atlanta—and quite possibly the ultimate use of cute in a commercial enterprise.

Being a Julianna pig from Holland, Sophie is extremely well bred. She sports a different bandana or frock every day, and never, ever comes to work without her jewelry. Like any cultured swine, she prefers pearls, but will also wear diamonds and blue topaz.

Miss Sophie dines primarily on sweet horse feed and fruit, but prefers Cheetos, raisins, bananas, and rice cakes. She is fully housebroken—it took her only 48 hours to learn—and she suffers no apparent ill effects from her toilet training. She loves to take showers to keep her trim, 50-pound svelte figure fresh smelling and clean.

She is definitely an indoor pig, making her position at the Sophisticated Swine a labor of love. The gift shop features jewelry, belts, handbags, hats, and jackets as well as home accessories and paintings.

Miss Sophie is at the shop Tuesdays through Saturdays from 10 a.m. to 5 p.m. The boutique is located just behind The Public House at 589C S. Atlanta Street on the town square in historic Roswell. She epitomizes the old cliché, "A little swine makes the heart gay."

Up in Smoke

Barbeque is one of the great passions of the South. But even though the passion is shared throughout the region, each state has its own individual ways of cooking and serving it. If you know what kind of barbeque a Southerner prefers, you can probably guess the state they hail from.

In Memphis, they like their barbeque dry, flavored with a dry rub of herbs and spices. In Texas, it is cooked over mesquite instead of hickory. In Florida, it is always served with cole slaw.

In Georgia, it is served "pulled"—the meat has been stripped away from the ribs or bones—and usually served on a bun, as a sandwich. You can also order just a plate of pulled barbeque—chicken, pork, or beef. In Georgia, barbeque is also almost always served with Brunswick Stew, even though the latter is not barbequed.

You can get ribs in Atlanta, of course, but usually only at chains that have invaded the city from elsewhere—places like Damon's, which started in Columbus, Ohio. Damon's serves great ribs, but they are not true Georgia barbeque.

To be picky, you won't find true Georgia barbeque in any establishment that has table linen or any other sign of refinement. True barbeque is cooked outdoors. If that is not feasible, then it is cooked in a shack. The closer the restaurant comes to resembling a shack, the more authentic the product is apt to be.

This is why you see signs touting "Real Pit Barbeque" on almost every barbeque restaurant in business. To Southerners, this claim means that the pork or beef or chicken has been cooked on a wood fire (hickory is preferred) since the beginning of time—or at least last evening.

You can find establishments that meet these criteria tucked here and there in the heart of Atlanta, but it is hard for downtown locations to maintain the state of collapse which is the hallmark of true barbeque. So for the authentic barbeque experience, it will be necessary to travel out of town. You can find good barbeque at the Fresh Air Barbeque on Route 23 in Jackson, as well as at Chad's, at the intersection of Routes 306 and 369 near Lake Lanier.

The best barbeque we have tasted, though, is at Hester's, a country store on Providence Road between Crabapple and Canton (a mile east of Route 140.) At Hester's, they cook the pork outdoors, in a big ole metal smoker, and you can eat it outdoors, too, if you wish—at one of their picnic tables. The pork is superb, the beans are deliciously distinctive, and the cole slaw and potato salad are fresh and zesty. The price is easy to swallow, too.

They've got cute signs, too.

The Underground

He looks real, sitting on the fountain, but he's a sculpture.

What does a city do with one of the largest railroad depots in the country, once passenger service has been eliminated by the ever-increasing public fascination with the friendly skies?

Atlanta has a pretty impressive answer to this question. It is called Underground—a collection of stores, shops, and restaurants which helps keep Downtown hot and kicking long into the evening.

Technically, Underground is both underground and aboveground. It is also the heart of Atlanta—the site where the fabled stake was driven into the ground 155 years ago, determining the end point of the proposed Western & Atlantic railroad.

As the railroad hub grew into a town, and then a city, an elaborate complex was built up to serve both the railroad companies and their customers. The underground parts served as boarding and loading areas for the trains; the aboveground areas served as ticket counters, waiting areas, and so on.

MARTA and The New Georgia Railroad still use some of the underground track areas, but much of the rest of the old complex has been transformed into one of Atlanta's most interesting retail and restaurant zones.

The Underground underlies Alabama St. and runs between Peachtree and Washington. It is next to the World of Coca-Cola and adjacent to the Five Points MARTA station. It is so easy to get to, in fact, that there is no reason to miss it on any visit to Atlanta.

The first order of business should be just to stroll through the whole place, to get a feel for it. There are three different levels to the Underground, with passageways running in many directions. Unless you orient yourself first, you may miss some of it.

One of the striking features of the Underground are the sculptures positioned here and there. The first one many people see is that of an old man sitting on the edge of a massive fountain wall. At first, he looks fully human, but as you study him you realize he is cast from metal.

There are other similar sculptures placed inconspicuously through the Underground. A favorite is the man with the dancing bear.

At busy times, there are usually a number of live shows being performed as well. A magician

An old truck becomes a kiosk for "Leftorium"

At Groundhog Tavern

may be entertaining the passersby with card tricks; a mime may stroll among the stalls, poking folks in their funny bones. You might even be able to get your fortune read!

There are two kinds of stores in the Underground: pushcarts, which deal with a very specialized product, and full stores, which are pretty much like their counterparts in any mall. The full scale stores include a Warner Bros. outlet with all kinds of souvenirs relating to their Looney Tunes cartoon characters, a Doubleday bookstore, Alamo Flags, Victoria's Secret, and a Wolf camera shop.

Kenny's Alley

The pushcarts tend to deal mostly in souvenirs, with a heavy emphasis on tee shirts. Many of these carts have been built to resemble locomotives and railroad cars. The Atlanta Committee for the Olympic Games has a couple of pushcarts at which they sell tee shirts, umbrellas, golf shirts, and other items bearing the Olympics 1996 logo. In addition, there are carts hawking left-handed items, novelties, and gift items.

The restaurants at the Underground make it a popular place for lunch as well as dinner. Anchor restaurants would be Damon's, on the upper level; Lombardi's, across from Kenny's Alley; City Harbor, which specializes in seafood; and the ever-popular Mick's. More spicy tastes can be found at the Caribbean Sunset, Malibu Jacks, and Tortilla Flats. Owl fans can be comforted at Hooter's.

Bugs and Sylvester wait to greet you.

One of our favorites is The Groundhog Tavern in Kenny's Alley. The sandwiches are overstuffed and fixed to perfection. Specific favorites include the California Club sandwich and a roast pork sandwich prepared Cuban style. Both were excellent. Connoisseurs of cuteness will also appreciate the man-size stuffed groundhogs permanently seated near the entrance to the Tavern.

The Underground really gets cooking as the night falls and folks filter in to hear the performers playing at various clubs. The best known is Dante's Down the Hatch, which features live soft jazz every night of the week. The interior of Dante's has been built to resemble a galleon from seafaring days gone by; it offers a light menu of excellent fondues as well as a full range of drinks.

City Harbor Seafood also offers live jazz on Friday and Saturday evenings.

Mittie's Tea Room

Mittie's is a restaurant that is easy to overlook. For one thing, it is only open from 11:30 to 2:30 Monday through Saturdays—and unless you arrive before noon or after 1:30, you can expect a wait. For another, it is small. Only about 25 customers can be seated at one time. And for a third, it is out of the way, located in a loft above two antique stores on Canton Street in Roswell.

But if you like good food for lunch, this is the one place not to overlook. It has everything you could ask for: quaintness, great food, and marvelous service.

Let's start with the quaintness. The upstairs loft used to be the projection booth of a movie theater. You have to go into the two stores that share the downstairs and then up a flight of steps to reach Mittie's.

The name Mittie is borrowed from Mittie Bulloch, a daughter of one the leading families that settled Roswell. She left Roswell in order to marry Theodore Roosevelt. Sr. The President of the U.S. bearing that name was their son.

It is not for the quaintness that the faithful line up to lunch at Mittie's, however. It is for the food. This is the domain of Rose Massaconi, who runs the restaurant with her husband Mitch.

Everything we tasted that came out of Rose's kitchen sent us into ecstasies. Few establishments have impressed us as much as this little tea room.

There are freshly made soups every day. We tried a cream of asparagus soup which was first rate (and served hot), as well as a chilled berry soup, which was obviously served cold. The berry soup blended various berries with a yogurt base. It was delicious.

For the main course, we chose a Mexican pie and a chicken salad sandwich, which is affectionately called "Mittie's."

The Mexican pie was something akin to a corn soufflé topped with tradtional Mexican accompaniments. It was a huge hit. The chicken salad was served on a buttery croissant and was billed as "our famous chicken salad." To whatever extent this fame has spread, it is well deserved. The white meat chicken is blended with toasted almonds and red seedless grapes and mixed with a wonderful tarragon mayonnaise with a hint of honey. It is clearly the best chicken salad we have yet to sample.

Incidentally, this was one of the few restaurants where we were tempted to try the iced tea. Iced tea in restaurants is usually made with inferior teas, then camaflouged with far too much sweetening. But, we reasoned, if you can't order iced tea in a tea room, where can you order it?

We were glad we did. It comes with a sprig of mint and is a perfect refreshment. Refills are free.

Be sure to leave room for dessert. Rose's carrot cake ranks among the best we've tasted; we also tried a blueberry and chocolate torte that was sublime.

On the last Saturday of each month, Rose and Mitch also open for dinner—a five-course meal on an international theme. Coming themes are Latin American dinner, a French dinner, an Italian dinner, and a Russian dinner. Reservations usually must be made more than a month in advance. Dress is casual, as it is for lunch.

Mittie's Tea Room is at 944 Canton Street, a half block from where Atlanta Street (Roswell Road closer to Atlanta) splits like a Y into Canton on the left and Alpharetta Highway on the right.

Mitch brings refills of iced tea to a party of four.

It Ain't Easy Bein' Sleazy

Every night from 10 p.m. on, you can hear the music from just about anywhere you happen to be on Highland Avenue. It blasts forth from Blind Willie's, a blues and jazz dive which may just be the hottest place in Atlanta, luring passersby to the front door. Just standing there, talking with the doorman, you can get a sample of the type of music being played that night. If you want more than a sample, though, it will cost you—the cover charge varies from $8 to $12.

Mighty Joe Houston

Whether you are a connoisseur of the blues or just a tourist looking for a memorable evening, the entertainment will definitely be worth it. Impressario Eric King has a keen eye for talent, and fills his bill with such headliners as Mighty Joe Houston, Johnny Clyde Copeland, Houserocker Johnson, and Honeyboy Edwards. There is usually a solid opening act band as well, such as the Shadows or the Excellos.

The motto of this establuesment is "It ain't easy bein' sleazy," and both the bar and the performers manage to carry this idea to the fullest each and every night. The bar opens at 8 each night and stays open as long as the good times continue to roll on, into the early morning hours. The music is limited to the juke box most nights until 10, although the action will start at 9 and again at 11 if the headliner is making a rare, two-set appearance.

The night we visited, The Shadows were the set-up band. They played mostly what they called "Swamp Blues"—they are cajun born and bred—but occasionally tossed in an Otis Redding tune to pacify the Georgia crowd. They were plenty hot; the wood floorboards in the bar began to vibrate with music, creating a giant blues sounding board that made every molecule in your body jump with the blues. This is not just music to listen to; you absorb it and become one with it.

But The Shadows were just that compared with the main attraction, Mighty Joe Houston, who began his set—to an SRO crowd—just before midnight. Billed as a "honkin', shoutin' sax maniac," he was every bit of that and more. As he walked toward the stage, he seemed to be just a demure, little black man from Austin. But the moment he started singing and playing, he ignited the whole place—the stage, the bar, the entire Virginia Highlands neighborhood. He scorched and stomped his way through number after number, gaining in intensity with every one.

The Shadows play the blues under a watchful eye on the right

Blind Willie's offers "blues, booze, and Cajun food," in that order. The menu is limited to Po Boy sandwiches and chicken wings.

If you are in the mood for the hottest music in town, check out Blind Willie's, at the sign of the singing crocodile at 828 N. Highland Ave. For information on who's playing, dial 873-BLUE.

Southern Fried Pizza

There may well be some things that are better off *not* left to the imagination. At the top of the list: what would pizza taste like if it had been developed in the South, rather than Italy?

First, the crust would be made of grits. The sauce would be made of green tomatoes instead of red. The toppings would be such things as salt-cured ham, okra, catfish filets, and squash. The whole thing would then be smothered with sausage gravy.

Actually, even this would probably be better than some pizzas we have tried. In our book, tofu is not a legitimate pizza topping. But this little excursion into the Pepto-Bismol division of the imagination does illustrate a point.

Pizza is not an authentic dish of Southern cooking.

And Atlanta does not yet have a first-class pizza—a deficiency which we hope will be corrected in the near future.

Please do not misunderstand. There are indeed many restaurants in Atlanta that serve a very good pizza. Most of these, however, are "designer" pizzas—pizzas that are made with sun-dried tomatoes, Cajun shrimp, and other exotic ingredients, then cooked in a hearth.

One of the best of this upper crust of pizza is served at Rocky's, who have two locations—one on Peachtree in the Buckhead corridor, and the other on Roswell Road in Sandy Springs. The result is something so good that it must be eaten by candlelight. But is it pizza? Not when a dinner for two ends up costing $25 to $30.

Pizza is supposed to feed a family of four for less than $20. It is supposed to be made of pepperoni and mushrooms. If you are a big spender, you might add olives or sausage—but the whole point of pizza is its simplicity and its low cost.

And—you ought to be able to get it delivered.

Of course, it should also taste good, and this is the nub of our sad story. The inexpensive pizza scene in Atlanta is dominated by the big pizza chains—Dominos, Pizza Hut, and Little Caesar. These are outfits that traditionally spend more time worrying about getting the pizza to you in 30 minutes or less than in trying to bake a good pizza. We keep trying them, of course, hoping for a miracle. Dominos is occasionally acceptable. But most of the time, we are disappointed.

Fellini's, in Buckhead, does serve up a very good pizza. But this is a small chain, focused primarily in the trendy North inside the Perimeter. They don't deliver in Smyrna or Alpharetta.

If Atlanta can draw the Olympics, we surely ought to be able to invoke a really good, cheap pizza. It's just a matter of closing ranks and asking in the right places.

In this instance, that happens to be the great god Pepperoni (Ronny, for short). Light a votive candle at his shrine (a leftover piece of pizza will do) every morning and ask that he grant us all a boon—a pizza that is priced right, tastes great, and is readily available throughout metro Atlanta.

Of course, if you are the kind of person who would put a Big Foot in your mouth, this crusade is not for you. It is a quest for perfect pizza purity.

Outdoor dining at Fellini's Pizza

Gabe's

There are many elements which must come together to make a wonderful restaurant. Good food. A creative chef. The right location. A charming atmosphere. Skilled waiters. And an owner or manager who will accept nothing less than perfection.

Gabe's Lodge in Roswell has it all, and then some. It is a perfect spot for a romantic night on the town.

This is a restaurant with history. As the story goes, the building has been around since before the Civil War, when it was being used as a Masonic Lodge. It was saved from Sherman's pyromania due to the fact that the general was a Mason, too. This is perhaps more embellishment than fact, since Sherman left the fate of Roswell in the hands of one of his deputies.

In any event, Gabe had already estabished himself as a restauranteur in Buckhead (Gene & Gabe's Upstairs) when he purchased this old building on Canton Street, at its intersection with Alpharetta Highway. He stripped the walls and floors down to the originals, then began rebuilding, reshaping, and recreating. The result is warm, cozy—inviting.

In warm weather, the place to dine is upstairs, on the balcony porch. From there, you can watch the traffic scurrying to and fro on Canton Street, yet stay above the fray. On chilly evenings, the optimum spot is on the first floor, at one of the tables next to the warm fire sparking away in the hearth.

We sampled two of the appetizers, both of which were excellent. One was a special for that night, consisting of asparagus topped with crumbled croutons and grated Parmesan cheese. It was outstanding. The second was roasted red peppers topped with thick slabs of provolone cheese, served with olives and hot peppers on a leaf of red leaf lettuce. It was similarly delicious.

The appetizers were followed by a very good house salad, served with excellent breads and an "Italian caviar" spread of chopped olives. A wonderful herb butter accompanied the breads.

The specialty at Gabe's is the veal. According to our waiter, Gabe hand cuts the veal himself, assuring the highest quality and freshest meat. There is no question that the veal was the most tender, smoothest veal we have ever tried. And there are about seven to eight different ways the chef will fix it for you. We tried three of them—topped with a pesto sauce (which was a special for that evening), sautéed with prosciutto ham and lemon, and sautéed with Marsala and mushrooms. All were excellent. They will also serve veal with an Amaretto cream, with artichoke hearts, and in a number of other ways.

Gabe's offers a range of pasta dishes, chicken, fish, and steaks and chops as well.

The veal dishes were served with either a side of spaghetti, a potato croquette, or sautéed zucchini. The potato croquette is one of the signature dishes of the restaurant—and it lives up to its billing. It is wonderful.

Gabe always has a number of homemade desserts to tempt his diners. We tried a special one he fixes in tribute to Georgia: a peach that is grilled and then sauced to perfection. One of our party also tried a sorbet that had been splashed with spumanti. On earlier visits, we have also indulged in a tiramisu that is wonderful.

To top it off, we had a cup of cappuccino, brewed and infused to perfection. It was a fine way to end a delicious meal.

Our server was attentive, knowledgeable, and very helpful. It is clear that everyone in the place is proud to be associated with Gabe's—and rightly so. We thoroughly enjoyed ourselves.

Reservations can be made at 993-7588.

Reaching the Apex

A sketch of the new Apex

The history of the black experience in America since slavery is not just the saga of struggle that typifies the usual reports. It is also a story of success, achievement, sharing, artistic development, and philanthropy.

The Apex Museum in the heart of Atlanta has dedicated itself to telling the fuller fabric of the black story. It calls itself "the museum of pride," because it focuses on the accomplishments of blacks and the black community.

The goal is to become a tribute to international black achievement. But the museum has not tried to embrace the whole international spectrum at once. Instead, it has chosen to start with what it knows well—the tight-knit community of Auburn Street in Atlanta which was the heart of worldwide black success for many decades.

Visitors to Apex begin with a trolley ride back in time. While sitting on seats designed to look like a trolley on Auburn Street, you are shown a film about "Sweet Auburn" and the people who shaped it into a symbol for black success during the first half of this century. Narrated by Cicely Tyson and Julian Bond, this is one of the best short films shown at the various museums and attractions around Atlanta. It does not just tell a story; it sets a tone. It invites you to experience Auburn Street with those who lived there years ago.

The museum also features a recreation of the first black-owned drugstore in Atlanta, right down to the packets of aspirin. Other displays highlight artifacts from other early black businesses.

The main hall of the museum is reserved for showings of black art. These shows change on a regular basis, bringing in outstanding black artwork from all over the globe.

Presently, the museum is limited by the space available to it. Plans have been launched to build a new building next door, in which the museum can grow to its own apex. It should be ready in time for the Olympics.

This is a charming, small museum which deserves to be supported by the whole community, so that it can grow in size and importance. Its basic ideals of reaching for the top—and then sharing that achievement with others—constitute a message that everyone can be inspired by.

The Apex does what all museums ought to do—it draws you into the experience of days gone by.

The Apex museum—the name is an acronym for "African American Panoramic Experience"—is located Downtown at 135 Auburn Avenue, just east of Courtland.

Behind the counter at the drug store.

Home in the Dome

The first Super Bowl was played during the first season of the Atlanta Falcons as an NFL franchise. The Falcons did not expect to make it to the Super Bowl that first year—but neither did they expect to be shut out of the big prize for 26 additional seasons.

This year, the Super Bowl is coming to Atlanta—but not because the Falcons have any better chance of being a part of it than in any other season. The Super Bowl is coming to Atlanta because the city boasts a brand new dome.

The whole world will see the dome during the Olympics, of course, when it will be one of the venues for the games. But why wait two years to showcase something this spectacular?

And spectacular it is—not to mention slightly unsettling. It may be hopelessly old-fashioned, but there is something a little eerie about playing football indoors on a plastic rug. The players hit each other, dive for balls, and generally raise havoc—and yet their uniforms remain spotless. How can this possibly be the same game that was played by Bronco Nagurski?

It is also slightly disconcerting to see huge men run up and down the field for a couple of hours, yet hardly break a sweat—even though the temperature in Atlanta is 90° plus. That's the temperature outside the dome. Inside, the temperature is a constant 70°, comfortable both for the fans and the players.

Which brings up the question: why build a dome for football in Atlanta, where snow comes once a year and almost never during football season?

The answer: you can raise a lot more hell in a closed dome than an open stadium And the one element of NFL games that never comes across on television, no matter how big your screen may be, is the high decibel level of the noise generated, not just by the fans but by the home team's management.

An NFL game is not a convention of Amway

Jerry Glanville confers with a player; Eric Dickerson scampers through a big hole.

Rison catches the ball, but is unable to land inbounds, even with help of a feathery friend

sales people—although 70,000 of them did pack the dome not too long ago. It is organized mayhem. Orchestrated bellicosity.

Actually, it is hard to tell whether it is a football game or a rock concert. In response to the guidance coming over the megahertz sound system, the audience stomps and screams and cheers from the opening kickoff to the final gun. The resulting roar rises heavenward—only to hit the top of the dome and bounce back into the stadium, creating a deafening din. Without the dome, the noise level would be only a fraction of what it is.

Unfortunately, NFL games are not won by noise level alone. It is also necessary to field a team that can win. And this is where the Falcons have struggled. In 27 seasons, they have made the playoffs just four times, and have never made it past the second round.

The 1993 season has gotten off to an especially lackluster start, with a string of losses.

The fans, however, do not seem to care. They continue to flock in to see the Falcons play, filling the dome for almost every game that has ever been played here. The team has responded to this encouragement, winning two-thirds of its home games over the past two seasons. But the good showing at home has not compensated for a less-than-stellar record on the road.

TV shoots the action

Still, the Falcons do have the capacity to be an exciting team. With Bobby Hebert joining Chris Miller and Billy Joe Tolliver at quarterback this year, the Falcons have one of the strongest trios of quarterbacks in the league. Receiver André Rison has the ability to break loose and score on any pass play. And of course anytime Deion Sanders fields a punt or a kickoff, he is a threat to take it back all the way. He owns almost half of the Falcon's records for longest kick returns, including two returns of more than 100 yards.

The talent is there—it is just a question of coach Jerry Glanville putting it together so that it performs consistently. He reached his first milestone in 1991, when they reached the playoffs. But the Falcons must learn to fly higher if they are to reach the Super Bowl.

The Varsity

When McDonald's opened its first store in Moscow a few years ago, it made a big deal out of how large it was and how many thousands of people it served in a single day.

Tell it to The Varsity, a fast food emporium that has served thousands of Atlantans every day for 50 years from its single location in Midtown, just across the interstate from Georgia Tech.

So many folks have eaten at The Varsity during its very successful lifetime that it is, hands down, the most famous restaurant in Atlanta—more famous than the dining room at the Ritz Carlton, more famous than anything at the Underground, even more famous than Hooters.

Even more amazing, it has made its reputation selling hamburgers, hot dogs, french fries, and onion rings. All cooked in oil. In a day and age of low-fat consciousness, The Varsity is not just a throw back to a day gone by. It is a daily statement that people do not want yogurt and bean sprouts. They want junk food.

The truth of this statement is attested to by the sheer size of The Varsity. It covers an entire block of downtown Atlanta. It is the only restaurant that we have ever encountered that has actually built its own two-level parking garage to handle the vast numbers that come to buy its wares.

Like any fast food place, you place your order at the counter—a huge hallway that always seems to resemble a MARTA car at rush hour rather than a food service area. The hamburgers and hot dogs are all precooked. Once you place your order, it is assembled to your specifications, reheated, and then presented to you. As many as six different people may be involved in putting it all together, but this is typical of the aura of confusion that reigns at The Varsity. Somehow, miraculously, it all comes together perfectly.

From there, you can take your order back to the office—or you can fan out to one of a half dozen huge dining rooms where you can wolf down your feast. Television is offered in one of the rooms, for those who cannot digest a hot dog without electronic assistance.

The food? The onion rings were excellent; the french fries are quite good. The hamburger was on a par with McDonald's. We did not try the hot dog (or any of its many toppings), but friends who have swear by it.

The secret of success? The price is incredibly cheap.

It's a formula that has kept Atlantans coming back for fifty years.

Shootin' the Hooch

Way up north, sensible people travel each summer even further north, into the backwoods of Canada, so that they can paddle—and portage—canoes across that country's vast, pristine lakes.

Life is much simpler in Atlanta. Thanks to the Chattahoochee River, which embraces the western boundary of the city while it snakes its way through the metro area, an hour or two—or a whole day—of canoeing is right in our backyard.

If you are the kind of person who finds canoeing too ambitious, you can rent an inner tube or a raft and let the river carry you downstream.

Of all the possible ways of discovering Atlanta, this may be the tops. The river is generally calm and placid. As you float or paddle along, you see trees and shrubs and natural wildlife, rather than strip centers, gas stations, and the MARTA. There are no street signs to advise you where you are; soon, the illusion is complete. You feel as though you were in a different world.

This is Atlanta as it was 175 years ago, before it became a large metropolis. Well, almost as it was. The bridges for Georgia 400 and Roswell Road weren't there. And not even all of the river was there; the Morgan Falls dam has widened this stretch of the river considerably—as have other dams elsewhere.

In Cherokee, the word "Chattahoochee" means something akin to "glistening stones." As you glide along the banks in early morning, with the fog still clinging to the water's surface in the cooler areas, it is easy to speculate on why they named it so. Perhaps the glistening stones were not rocks at all, but fellow travelers emerging out of the mists, their canoes glistening in the sunlight.

Atlanta is a city full of potential. The river that runs along its edge feeds the imagination, if you take the time to explore it and discover its mysteries. As the waters flow south to the Gulf of Mexico, they refresh the soul of Atlanta and keep it forever young, full of hope. An hour or two shootin' the Hooch can likewise refresh your imagination.

If canoeing or rafting is not for you, then at least explore the parks that stretch along the river's edge for most of the 48 miles from Standing Peachtree to Lake Lanier. Or come out and watch a rowing club practice for a race.

Canoes, tubes, and rafts can be rented by the hour from Chattahoochee Canoe and Raft Rental on Azalea Drive just west of Roswell Road.

Joe Oliver places a canoe into the Chattahoochee.

The Nature Center

Why did the kingfisher cross Willeo Road?

To get his broken wing fixed by the good folks at the Chattahoochee Nature Center, of course.

In fact, all kinds of birds end up being treated and healed at the center, which has been a friend to wildlife—and humans—since it began operating 17 years ago.

On the boardwalk

Once the birds are healed, they are released back into the wild, if at all possible. Only those birds which cannot make it in the wild—like a blind owl—become permanent residents at the center.

"We do not have animals on display, as a zoo might," explains Karen Menton of the center. "But if an animal must be kept here permanently, we do let our visitors view them." This includes a large aviary.

Even though the center specializes in birds, it is not limited by this preoccupation. In fact, the work with birds is kept largely in the background, as a pet project. As far as the general public is concerned, the Chattahoochee Nature Center is a wonderful spot to interact with some of the more unusual aspects of nature.

This interaction occurs in three ways: 1) through the educational displays and exhibits at the lodge, 2) along the woodlands trail, and 3) along the wetlands boardwalk.

The lodge houses the center itself. There are a number of excellent exhibits here, plus a few unusual ones—a stuffed Georgia bear and a huge preserved turtle which children are encouraged to touch. Adjacent to the lodge are numerous aviaries in which rare species of hawks and eagles that cannot be returned to the wild are kept.

Across a small lake from the center is the beginning of the Woodlands Trail, a short trail along the lake and then up a small hillside through the forest. Significant features along the trail have been numbered. By reading the matching number in the brochure you are given when signing in at the lodge, you can learn a great deal about natural Georgia habitats.

By far the most fascinating feature of the center, though, is the Wetlands Trail. It starts across Willeo Road from the lodge, right at the edge of the Chattahoochee River! The trail is actually a boardwalk that leads you right into the heart of the reeds and swamp that compose the ecologic environment along the river's edge. Once again, numbered stations let you read about the plants and habitats you are viewing, as you follow the boardwalk along its trail.

At the far end of the boardwalk is a lean-to shelter which lets you sit down and contemplate the wonders of life along the Chattahoochee. From there, the boardwalk meanders back to-

The Chattahoochee, as viewed from the boardwalk

Ducks enjoy a swim in the nature center's lake; a staffer shows off one of the resident snakes

ward its starting point. The tour of the wetlands provides a miniature class in the development of a marsh, and how it changes with the seasons.

This is one of the great treasures to be found in Atlanta.

In fact, the whole nature center deserves patronage and support. The total property embraces 125 acres of prime waterfront land in Roswell. Another 75 acres are to be added next year. Together, the center makes a wonderful teaching center for metro area students.

The center also sponsors a number of novel programs, such as the Halloween Hike—which is presented as a wholesome alternative to the typical haunted house. The Woodland Trail is lit to guide hikers to mystical creatures and plants that will then talk about themselves and the environment.

An ongoing program is the Evening Float, which is held on Wednesday evenings throughout the summer (and into fall). The Float is a two-hour canoe excursion along the river's edge to get an up close and personal view of herons, beaver, and other wildlife. It requires advance registration and is restricted to people eight years and older.

The staff naturalists also regularly arrange field trips for the more hardy explorers—one day canoe trips in north Georgia or weekend trips to the barrier islands along the Georgia coast. A one-day trip scheduled for this November is a Native American history tour to New Echota and other Cherokee sites in north Georgia—although the center is quick to point out that even the Indians were not Georgia's original natives. The bears and owls and snakes and frogs and kingfishers were.

The Chattahoochee Nature Center is located at 9135 Willeo Road in Roswell. Follow Roswell Road north through Sandy Springs. Immediately after crossing the Chattahoochee, turn left on Azalea Drive. Follow Azalea Drive until it dead ends into Willeo. Turn left on Willeo and follow it to the nature center.

The Nature Center is a nonprofit corporation that depends on fees and sales to survive. If you use the trails, please sign in at the lodge first and pay the nominal fee. Another good way to help the center is to patronize the gift shop in the front room of the center. It is well stocked with bird feeders, bird seed, nature books, nature toys, and other novel items.

Not all of Atlanta is hustle and bustle. Fortunately, there are places like the Chattahoochee Nature Center to escape to—and find the true Atlanta again.

In the gift shop

A Pleasant Diversion

Why do artists usually view the nude as the ultimate challenge of their skill? Is it because they have a prurient need to ogle naked women? Or is it because they see a level of beauty and grace in the nude that they cannot find anywhere else?

Why do Americans get so jittery whenever the subject of nudity arises? In Europe, nudity is commonplace on television and in the theater. Most folks do not think anything more about it than having a glass of wine with dinner. It is normal, healthy—even refreshing.

In America, however, we make a federal case out of it—literally. We run to the courts and ask them to ban this book, close down that movie, or prohibit a nude bar from operating in our neighborhood. Like the little boy who cried wolf,though, we have begun to wear down the patience of the courts.

In Atlanta, the battle lines seem to be drawn over all-nude show bars. The courts have ruled that they are legal under the laws of Georgia, and that even zoning laws cannot be used to keep them out of a neighborhood—if other legal businesses are allowed to operate in the area.

These rulings have led to the opening of a goodly number of show bars, most of which seem to be operating successfully. Judging from the number of cars in the parking lots of various show bars, they are indeed highly popular.

Kudzu Undercover decided that this guide to what is hot in Atlanta would be incomplete without an investigation into this hot, hot topic. Curiously, it was not difficult to find volunteers for this assignment.

We chose to visit the Mardi Gras, a medium-sized show bar located just behind the Wendy's at the Powers Ferry exit of I-285 on the northwest side of town.

Actually, the Mardi Gras is a hybrid—part show bar and part sports bar. There are numerous big screen televisions that are tuned to sporting events, and then there are a handful of stages where the dancers dance.

They start out each dance wearing at least as much as most women wear to the beach. As the dance progresses, the tops and bottoms come off—usually because someone in the audience has encouraged the dancer to do so, by slipping a dollar or two into the garter she wears on one thigh. The dancing is no different than it would be if they had their clothes on.

If a member of the audience is a big spender, he will tip the dancer $5 or $10. She will then do one dance tableside or tabletop for the customer. It is something like a violinist strolling table to table in an Italian restaurant—except that at the nude bar, no fiddling is allowed.

The Mardi Gras also features a buffet table both at lunch and dinner.

Contrary to the fears of clergy and uninformed wives, the audience is well behaved. The atmosphere resembles that of a neighborhood bar, which it is, far more than a den of iniquity.

As for the fear that the ogling of previously forbidden territory will pervert people, it seems baseless. The day we were there, a Braves-Giants game was being broadcast on the big screen. All eyes were glued on the TV—almost no one was watching the dancers. Mark Lemke was proving to be a hotter item than a bunch of dancing nudes.

It's a pleasant diversion from such nasty realities as a sagging economy. And it is unquestionably good for Atlanta as a convention city. Perhaps by the time of the Olympics we can even become sufficiently cosmopolitan as to have full scale revues à la the Folies Bergère.

A Good Ole Truck

As with so many issues, the question of what Atlantans drive depends on where they live. Inside the Perimeter, it will be a late model car, probably an import. Outside the Perimeter, it will be a pickup truck.

Southern men and women take their trucks

seriously. The kind of truck they drive, and what they haul in it, becomes part of their self-expression. It establishes their stature in the community.

In fact, it is common to see pickups in suburban driveways. Many Southerners own them even though they have no real need for one. It's a status thing—a place you can hang your gun rack.

In Europe, there is a saying, "Mercedes owns the road." It refers to the fact that owners of Mercedes-Benzes inevitably drive as though they were lord and master of the highway. In the South, people who drive pickups behave the same way. If you drive a truck, it seems as though—

- All normal traffic laws and speed limits have been suspended for you—but not for anyone else.
- You always have the right of way.
- People who drive cars must love to dodge errant trucks, since they have so much practice.
- The back of a pickup truck is a great place to haul your kids. (Believe it or not, this practice is illegal in other states.)

Of course, if you stray too far from Atlanta, you may encounter what is known as "farmer driving," the tendency to drive down the middle of a two lane country road, usually at high speed, until you see someone actually coming toward you. Then you return to your assigned lane—at least until the other vehicle has passed.

If you are not aware of this form of driving, however, you may not realize that the truck is going to return to his own lane before smashing into you. Indeed, you may be tempted to swerve out of his way, landing perhaps in a ditch, from which vantage point you are clearly able to see the pickup truck passing by—in his proper lane.

One last caution: never follow too closely behind a loaded pick-up, as there is a good chance part or all of the load will fall out. This is also true with larger trucks carrying pigs to market. The interstates down here are closed at least twice a year by liberated livestock, blocking hundreds of cars.

The roads of metro Atlanta are still pig trails, after all.

A Railroad Empire Still

The switching pen at the Norfolk and Southern yard in west Atlanta

Atlanta was conceived in the womb of the burgeoning railroad system in this country; it owes the first 100 years of its unparalleled growth to the rails as well. Atlanta quickly became the most important hub in the South—and one of the key distribution centers in the whole country.

In the last 50 years, however, the magic and romance of the rails has disappeared into a haze of nostalgia. Five Points is no longer host to thousands of intercontinental train passengers daily; it is now the heart of Atlanta's rapid transit system, MARTA. There is still passenger service on Amtrak to and from Atlanta, but it operates out of a tiny depot on Peachtree Road at I-85.

Few Atlantans even think about the railroads these days, or how much the city owes them. And yet the railroads, once a mighty empire, are still one, albeit of a different sort. They have lost the passenger travel to the airlines, it is true, but they still remain a king of moving freight throughout the country.

A caboose sits on a side track

Every day, hundreds of trains—each as long as 200 cars—chug their way in and out of Atlanta. They go to their system's yard, where the cars are separated and then reassembled into new trains, depending on their destination. The process is something like dealing cards. On a train 100 cars long, each car may be destined to a different city. As the train enters the system's yard, the cars are cut loose one by one. They roll into the switching pen,

A crane lifts a container off of a truck to load onto a train; this switch is thrown by computer

where a series of switches sends them into one of many tracks, where they will be assembled with other cars going to the same destination. When the new train is long enough, they will hook it to a locomotive and it will chug out of the yard, letting the rails take it to its next stop.

This is the way the railroads have been operating for years—or is it? In theory it is, but in practice the railroads are far more up to date than we realize. The inside of a railroad terminal tower looks a lot like an air control tower. The switching in the yard, for example, is all done by computer. Sophisticated television camera systems let the controllers monitor and inspect incoming trains without leaving the terminal building.

Whenever Atlanta's leaders talk with pride about transportation these days, it is usually to brag about Hartsfield. But let us not forget the railroads. They fueled this city's growth and are still a major economic force in its well-being.

Many rail systems still operate through Atlanta. One of the major players is Norfolk Southern; its Inman Yard just northwest of Downtown is control center for the entire Norfolk Southern system, which embraces 15,000 miles of track in 20 states. In Georgia alone, Norfolk Southern employs about 5,000 people.

Due to the danger involved, rail yards are not open for tours. Nonetheless, they continue to play a vital role in our daily lives—behind the scenes.

A train arrives in the yard; diesels wait to be serviced

The Holy Ghost

People come to the Atlanta area for many reasons. For Father Bob, one of the Trappist monks who lives at the Monastery of the Holy Spirit in Conyers, it was the essence of peace that first attracted him. He's lived here ever since.

The peace that pervades the monastery is undoubtedly much stronger today than when Father Bob first arrived—both within the monastery and within his heart. It has had a chance to develop and ripen, as the small band of monks built their community—a magnificent church, a cloister, a retreat, and grounds. Virtually all of the work was done by the brothers, including the creation of several lakes, which were dammed up with the aid of an army surplus bulldozer.

The courtyard inside the cloisters.

Like all monasteries, the monks have at times struggled to support themselves. They have tried various forms of farming, but bad crops have been a test of patience, faith, and perseverance. Over the years, however, a new kind of crop has emerged, one that took a while to recognize. This was the steady stream of people who came to visit the monastery, day after day. They came to see and to understand. They often came looking for spiritual nourishment. And when they left, they frequently wanted to take with them some tangible souvenir of their visit—to remind them of the peace they had felt. So the brothers started a small gift shop, selling some books, Catholic gift items, and products from other Trappist monasteries. They also started selling some of the bread they baked at the monastery.

The bread, especially, has been a big hit. Folks will come from miles around to stock up on it. Others will leave with just a loaf or two—at least until they taste it, and come back for more.

The monks also conduct a thriving business raising and selling bonsai plants and tools and pots for cultivating them. Bonsai plants are miniature trees and shrubs that have been carefully trained to look like full-grown, weather-worn

A decorative tile; Father Bob displays prize lotuses growing in the retreat's garden.

The bell tower; a statute of Christ blesses the cloister; and the magnificent sanctuary

trees, even though they are only a few inches tall. One bonsai planter can easily depict an entire landscape in miniature.

But the real product of the monastery is neither bread nor bonsai plants. It is peace—at least, the opportunity to find peace and learn to recreate it in your own life. As more and more visitors came to the monastery over the years, some of them wanted to stay—not as monks, but as visitors—until they felt refreshed or worked out some inner conflict. So the brothers built a visitor's retreat, where people can come and stay for a weekend or longer—to meditate, seek guidance, and restore themselves. Some come individually; others come as groups. The retreat center is open to people of all faiths, and it may just as easily be rented out by Buddhists as by Catholics. Priests are on hand if guidance is sought, but otherwise people on retreat are left to themselves—and God—to wander through the gardens, stroll along the lakes, read in the library, or just sort through their confusion.

Visitors are welcomed to come to the monastery at any time during the day—to pray or worship in the lovely church, to picnic by the lake (or feed the ducks), or to buy bread or plants at the gift shop. The monastery is located at 2625 Highway 212, a few miles south of the route 20 exit on I-20.

It's a beautiful place to find peace.

Ducks have found the perfect retreat; one of many bonsai plants awaiting adoption

Zoo Atlanta

Nothing seems to capture and hold the attention of kids quite as much as big, furry animals—unless it is small, slimy ones. Zoo Atlanta has them both, as well as a lot of other familiar and exotic animals.

A bear clowns around in his private pool

The zoo is located in the southern portion of Grant Park—which was not named for the northern general of that name, but for Lemuel Grant, a transplant Yankee who masterminded the building of fortifications around Atlanta during the Civil War.

Atlanta came by its zoo almost by chance. A traveling circus visited the city in 1889, only to end up in bankruptcy. In order to meet the claims of employees and suppliers, the circus sold its menagerie to a local businessman, who donated the animals to the city as the basis for a zoo.

Today, the zoo houses the primate collection of Emory University, an outstanding collection of gorillas and orangutans. It also has smaller displays of just about every type of wild animal.

The one drawback of the zoo is its limited space. With just 40 acres, there is only so much space for exhibits. As a result, the zoo is somewhat on the small side. But what the zoo staff has been able to do with its limited space is nothing short of spectacular. Zoo Atlanta is a true zoological garden. Far from being a succession of cages and pens, as it is in many zoos, Zoo Atlanta is a maze of interlocking paths through the African forest. Trees, shrubs, and plants native to the animals' habitats tower over the winding paths, so that you have the illusion of walking through a jungle or rain forest, not a city zoo. And there is a surprise around every bend in the path—a tiger, a giraffe, or a rhinoceros.

The native motif has been carried out expertly, right down to signs in the original native tongues of each area being recreated. Even the restrooms are covered with thatch and look like they've been transported from the jungle!

The most fascinating display is undoubtedly the gorilla section, where the famous Willie B. holds court over his harem. The gorillas can be observed through a large glass window in a very realistic replica of their native habitat. At times, however, it is easy to wonder who is studying whom, as the gorillas come up close to the window, squat down, and stare back at the crowd of fascinated humans on the other side of the pane.

The animals that are the most fun to watch

A giraffe, an elephant, and a cayman crocodile

The gate into Ketambe, a rain forest; a sea lion taking a breather from the cares of the day

tend to be the bears and the sea lions. The bear will bat around a large ball or soak in his hot tub size pool, much to the delight of the children and adults looking on. It is clear that the bear is something of a ham. So are the sea lions, who will bask belly-side up on the ledge of a partly-submerged rock—until one of the zookeepers comes by. Then they dart rapidly under water to see if the keeper is bringing food.

During the summer months (April through October), demonstrations are given several times a day on "birds of prey" and African elephants. Mini-ampitheaters are situated in appropriate areas throughout the zoo.

True to its origins, the zoo also features traveling displays. This past summer, it was a display of robotic dinosaurs.

The zoo also has a large petting zoo, which lets children get up close and personal with friendly animals such as sheep, llamas, and goats. When kids get tired of looking at animals, they can be entertained as well in a playground near the zoo entrance, riding on toys shaped like frogs and birds and other animals.

Kids, in fact, are the key to the zoo. During the summer, they come with their parents. When school is in, busload after busload of school kids line up each day for field trips. It is a wonderful laboratory for expanding the imagination and developing a sense of awe—and respect—for nature and the animal kingdom.

The zoo is close to Downtown and easy to reach. Heading east on I-20, take the Boulevard exit and head south on Boulevard. Turn right at your first opportunity, go one block to Cherokee, turn left and follow Cherokee until you come to the zoo entrance. Its proximity to Downtown and other attractions make the zoo a natural addition to the "must-see" list of tourists.

The Cyclorama, which houses a large, circular depiction of the Battle of Atlanta, is housed in a stately building just next to the zoo in Grant Park. There are separate admission fees for the zoo and the Cyclorama.

A busload of school kids swarm into the zoo; younger children play at the zoo playground

Buckhead Diner

If you are old enough to remember the old greasy spoon diners from the 40's and 50's, do not let the memories of these places prevent you from having dinner at the Buckhead Diner. It is a first-class operation in every respect—and a fun place to dine out. This opinion is supported, by the way, by a lengthy waiting line virtually every night of the week. It is wise, therefore, to come early—or dine late.

The Buckhead Diner has given itself the challenge of serving the same foods you might have ordered in a roadside diner 30 years ago—but preparing them as though they were gourmet dishes. As an example, they offer an appetizer called "Veal Meatloaf Sliders." A slider is an euphemistic term for a cheap hamburger served on a tiny bun like you would get at Krystal—or, up north, White Castle. Here, however, the meat is actually a thick slab of their veal meatloaf and the buns are freshly baked. The two sliders are served with a heaping pile of mashed potatoes in between. The end result bears almost no resemblance to the original slider—thank God! It is a perfect blend of tastes and makes an ideal appetizer.

Buckhead sliders

The veal meatloaf is also available as an entrée, without the buns.

We also tried the Tomato Fondue as a second appetizer. Served with crusty chunks of their homemade bread, it was excellent.

In keeping with the diner concept, Buckhead Diner features a blue plate special, which varies from night to night. The night we dined there, it was a mixed grill of smoked pork chops and barbeque chicken served with collard greens and peppered potatoes. Everything was superb.

Others at our table tried the spicy shrimp with linguini and the fresh grouper, which was served with potatoes and lima beans. The spicy shrimp lived up to its name—as did the jalapeño cole slaw which was ordered as a side. Do not order either one of these unless your fire insurance policy is paid up. They are definitely part of what makes Atlanta hot!

The grouper was at the opposite end of the scale, mild but sublime. The lima beans were the perfect counterpoint.

Two of us split a marvelous salad of asparagus, pine nuts, and goat cheese. The servers seem quite willing to split large orders such as the salads. In fact, the service was outstanding, even though the place was packed and every waiter was running around with more than enough to do.

We concluded our repast with a chocolate chip cheesecake, a white chocolate banana cream tart, and a peach bread pudding. We sank into ecstasy while we sipped a cup of coffee.

The Buckhead Diner is a great place to get excellent food at moderate prices. It is located on Piedmont in the heart of Buckhead, just opposite the dead end of East Paces Ferry.

It is one of a number of excellent restaurants run by the Buckhead Life Restaurant Group.

Nothing could be finer than dinner in the diner

More Than A Bookstore

Ideas. Ever since Plato first coined the word, we have kept ourselves busy dreaming them up, spinning off new ones, and, in general, trying to understand them.

We need ideas as much as we need oxygen. Without ideas—good ideas—life would be a simple contest of survival, nothing more. But with the capacity to work with ideas, we can probe the meaning of life, find fulfillment, and expand our horizons.

Books above, books below at Oxford

You can't walk into a store and buy an idea or two, the way you would buy an orange. But you can go into a bookstore and be surrounded by ideas—big ideas, great ideas, stupid ideas, and unworkable ideas. Thousands of them, maybe millions.

Atlanta is blessed by a great number of excellent bookstores. Today, bookselling is a high volume venture, and all of the big nationwide chains are here, some of them with superstores: Barnes & Noble, Borders, Waldenbooks, B. Dalton, and Little Professor.

But there is nothing quite as exciting as a one of a kind bookstore, a bookstore that has no copy of it anywhere. There is usually one in every big city. In Atlanta, it is the main Oxford Bookstore at 360 Pharr Road in Buckhead (they have two other locations as well).

Oxford sells books, but it is obvious that they see their mission as something more as well: nourishing the art of thinking—in fact, nourishing body, mind, and soul. They provide an excellent café for those who hunger for food as well as truth, complete with clever menu names such as "A Tale of Tunacity." There is also an extensive art gallery, in which they sell original artwork of all kinds; a video department, for those who prefer to watch rather than read; a comprehensive sheet music department; a comic books and T-shirts nook; and, of course, books—books on every subject imaginable.

Part of the art gallery on the second floor at Oxford

If you are the kind of person who believes great ideas are one of the hottest things around, spend an afternoon or evening at Oxford Bookstore. It sizzles.

Six Flags Over Georgia

Although Georgia already has had six—or is it seven?—state and national flags flying over it since its founding as a British colony, the flags in this attraction are not meant to ignite a political controversy. Six Flags Over Georgia is simply the name of a huge amusement park just across the Chattahoochee from Atlanta. It is called Six Flags Over Georgia because it is operated by the same folks who created Six Flags Over Texas—and that *was* a sentimental reference to Texas's unique history.

It really should be called Six Roller Coasters Over Douglasville. Whenever attendance shows signs of stagnating, they build yet another roller coaster, bigger and better than all the others, give it some exotic name such as the Great American Scream Machine or Ninja, and then dare everyone in Atlanta to see if they have the courage to ride it. Judging from the crowds that come out to Six Flags, a good many of the townspeople respond.

In between the roller coasters, there are all the other standard amusement park rides—a white water raft ride in huge rubber rafts; a giant water slide; a carousel which was originally built around the turn of the century and which has been carefully restored; and much more. FreeFall simulates the thrill (?) of falling from a ten-story building (with a parachute); if your death-wish survives that one intact, there is also the Great Gasp, which does the same thing from twice the height. A train circles the entire property, stopping periodically at old-fashioned depots named for local historical spots—Rabun, Marthasville, and so on.

Depending on the time of the year and the day of the week, there will also be a variety of shows presented in various parts of the park. A shoot-em-up oater is presented regularly in the Lick Skillet area, complete with loud gunshot sound effects. A diving demonstration, including a very, very high dive, is given frequently in the French section of the park.

For small children, there are milder attractions, such as Bugs Bunny Land.

At night, there are fireworks and a laser show, as well as concerts. During October, there is a 12-day festival called Fright Fest, which transforms the park into Six Ghouls Over Georgia. Kudzu sources report the Fright Fest is a truly superb haunted house.

The park is nicely laid out and landscaped. The weakest spot is in the food service, which is surprisingly limited

and not surprisingly expensive. You can usually find much better food at a state fair.

On the other hand, the park is well stocked with souvenir shops where parents can while away the time while their kids go for one more trip down Splashwater or another circuit on the Georgia Cyclone. One of the largest is a store selling T-shirts and cartoon memorabilia from Warner Bros. cartoons and movies. In fact, the entire Six Flags operation is now a division of Time Warner, and so we are apt to see more and more of "Six Flags Goes to the Movies" in the future.

On the whole, Six Flags Over Georgia succeeds quite well in what it sets out to do—create an amusement park on a grand scale. If you like thrills and excitement—or have a gaggle of kids who do—then you can easily spend the whole day at Six Flags and never run out of things to do.

Six Flags has its own exit off I-20 as you head west from Downtown. There is a charge for parking and admission, but once inside the gate, all the rides and programs are free.

Aunt Fanny's Cabin

Two long-standing traditions of Atlanta night life have merged to become a new force of entertainment at Aunt Fanny's Cabin, just outside the Perimeter in Smyrna.

The older tradition is the restaurant, Aunt Fanny's Cabin, which is reputed to be the oldest restaurant in metro Atlanta. It's not quite old enough to have been burned by Sherman, but its fame and reputation do go back more than 50 years.

Aunt Fanny's is a large place, designed to accommodate crowds. It is dedicated solely to the preservation and presentation of authentic Southern cooking—which means that there are just four items on the menu: fried chicken, Smithfield ham, catfish, and strip steak.

The fried chicken is excellent. Smithfield ham is a real venture into Southern cuisine. Unlike city hams, which are sugar cured, Smithfield ham is salt cured—a very much different taste. If you grew up eating country ham, you will love it.

The meat is accompanied by a squash casserole and macaroni and cheese, both of which were top notch, and a heapin' bowl of steamin' collard greens. The collard greens are much like the Smithfield ham; if you grew up eating them, you will be in seventh heaven.

Biscuits and cornbread are served with a tossed salad before the entrée arrives. Dessert is a homemade fruit cobbler. Although they were dry for a few months after changing ownership, they now have a full liquor license as well.

A vocalist and pianist perform in the main dining room every evening.

The second tradition is Gene Dale, who ran Upstairs at Gene and Gabe's in Buckhead for 13 years, and has now brought his production company to Aunt Fanny's. Every night Tuesday through Sunday, the lights dim at 8:30 and the curtain rises on one of his productions.

The current show is *Della's Diner—The Blue Plate Special,* a musical country soap opera, a free-wheeling, high kicking parody of soap operas. The action centers around Della, who owns a diner on top of Morning Glory mountain in Tennessee.

The lines are witty, the acting is inspired, the music is lively, and the songs are catching. In fact, we kept on humming the refrains from "Side of Fries" and "Morning Glory Mountain" for several days afterwards. If there had been an album, we would have bought it.

This is dinner theater at its best. Let's hope it is the beginning of yet another tradition.

Reservations for dinner, or dinner and the play, can be made at 436-5218. Aunt Fanny's is located at 2155 Campbell Road, just beyond the Perimeter.

Outlandish Landmarks

The best we can tell, these four cherished metro landmarks are meant to guide us safely to the land of whimsy. Such is certainly the case with the bridge at the Concourse, which has a boulder stuck into its apex. The tower at the Underground is, perhaps, a soaring reproduction of the stake that first demarcated Terminus. And what can be said for the residents of Marietta, who actually asked KFC to rebuild the denuded Big Chicken on Cobb Parkway, shown here, to its original, pristine, 50-ish condition. The Three Silos, near Crabapple, originally served a noble and utilitarian purpose. But the farm is gone, and now the towers are merely symbols of long-forgotten fertility.

Stone Mountain

You start with a big ole rock, about the size of a mountain. Stone Mountain, in fact, the largest outcropping of granite in the world. What do you do with it?

This was exactly the dilemma confronting the Venable family, who owned the big rock back at the turn of the century. So when they were contacted by Helen Plane with the idea of carving a memorial to the leaders of the Confederate cause, they deeded the north face of the mountain to the United Daughters of the Confederacy, provided they complete the work within 12 years.

The carving, as seen from Memorial Hall

Which they didn't. By 1928, the deadline, only the head of Robert E. Lee had been sculpted. So the Venables reclaimed the north face—and Lee's face as well.

The project remained undone until 1970. The state of Georgia bought the mountain in 1958. In 1963, it commissioned Walker Kirkland Hancock to complete the sculpture. Using jet torches to blast away stone, he completed the mammoth bas relief in eight years. Now, Jefferson Davis and Stonewall Jackson have joined Lee, and they are all gallantly riding horseback through the mists of memory.

The state has done more than just complete the carving, however; it has converted the 3200 acres around the mountain into a major state park and resort. The park features a skylift to the top of the mountain, a riverboat, a railroad, an antebellum plantation, an antique auto museum, a beach, and a petting zoo. The resort features an inn, a conference center, two daily fees golf courses, a carillon, and numerous restaurants.

Stone Mountain will provide several major venues for the 1996 Olympics, further enhancing its reputation as a premier recreational facility.

It can be reached by driving east from I-285 on U.S. Route 78.

An old mansion waiting for renovation; a riverboat waiting for passengers

The High Museum

The High Museum has had its own building at the Woodruff Arts Center for 10 years, with an extension at the Georgia-Pacific building Downtown. The High is still very much a growing museum searching for its full artistic mission; its promise shines forth radiantly in glorious pieces such as the Madonna and child

Once art leaves the easel, it departs the sphere of creativity and enters into the kingdom of Art Collectors—art museums, galleries, connoisseurs, and even people with lots of money and not quite as much taste. After this transition has been made, the work of art is not judged so much by its creative merit and message as by the consensual opinions of critics, collectors, and curators.

The artist is meant to serve the muse of Beauty, and his or her work should be judged as such. Collectors, alas, are often far less interested in beauty than in value and reputation.

Museums are usually caught in the middle. They promote public interest in art, but seldom deal directly with the artist; usually, they are at the mercy of art collectors and purveyors.

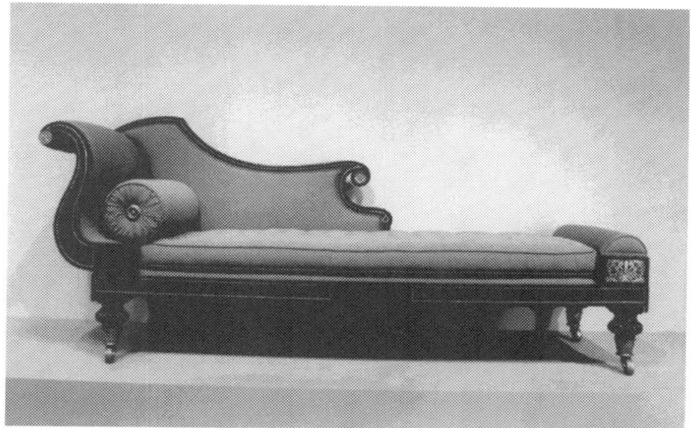

The High has a strong collection of furniture

The High Museum of Art has a good collection of art, but it needs to reinforce it with a few more truly great pieces—masterpieces that so capture your imagination that you are captivated by their sheer power and majesty and cannot move for a whole afternoon.

Devotees of contemporary art will argue that the High already has such pieces in its strong collection of modern art—the entire upper floor of the museum. But love for contemporary art is not a universally shared taste. For those who feel that much modern art is just expensive nonsense, lacking beauty if not style, the upper floor holds no such power.

The smaller displays of European and American art come closer, and offer much that is enjoyable and interesting. The same is true of the furniture as art collection, which may be the strongest collection at the High. The African folk art collection is a nice touch—but why not Southern folk art, too?

The High Museum of Art is located at 1280 Peachtree Street. A branch gallery is also located in the Georgia Pacific Center at 133 Peachtree.

Bigger than Scarlet?

Inside the CNN atrium

Ten years ago, Atlanta was most famous throughout the world for being the home of Scarlett O'Hara. Burnt Atlanta became a more vivid image in the minds of millions than rebuilt, prosperous, exciting Atlanta.

All of this has changed in the last few years, however. Now, the city of Atlanta is better known throughout the world for being the birthplace and headquarters of CNN—Cable News Network—than anything else.

This is no small achievement. At a time when television news was dominated by the three U.S. networks, Ted Turner took a gamble and introduced a 24-hour network which did nothing but broadcast the news. It was fed to televisions by cable.

It succeeded in large part because it could carry the news where the networks could not—to every country in the world. And because it was on the air 24 hours a day, it could deliver the news instantly, while it was still happening. It did not have to wait until 6:30 or 11 o'clock.

Due to the international success of CNN, its studios on International Boulevard have become one of the major attractions in Atlanta, especially among tourists from foreign countries, who are much more aware of Bernard Shaw than of Thomas Hood or William Sherman and the domestic brawl that brought them together 130 years ago.

CNN is aware of this interest and provides tours of the studios on a regular basis throughout each day. For $5 a person, the 45-minute tour takes you behind the scenes at CNN. The guide explains how Ted Turner, beginning in billboard advertising, developed WTBS into a national television "super station" and from that base took the leap into CNN, TNT, and the rest of his current projects.

There is ample time to oooh and aaah at Ted's many achievements, but there are also some fascinating looks "behind the scenes" at how a television news operation works.

It is important to be at CNN by 8 a.m. to get tickets for the tour, even for later in the day.

The CNN Center is built around a spacious atrium with a variety of fast food outlets, restaurants, and shops, making it a nice place to lunch.

The CNN tour begins with a video introduction

Ten Most Popular Tees

T-shirts have become popular throughout the country, but nowhere are they quite the high fashion item that they are in Atlanta. Perhaps it is the warm weather, which fits casual wear to a tee—or perhaps it is the heavy influence of athletics on the region. Whatever the cause, you can spot T- shirts anywhere, and the popular clothes item is sold everywhere imaginable, from the airport to the malls to roadside vendors.

The intriguing aspect of T-shirts is that they are more than clothes; they are part of our self-expression. They let us make a sociological statement as well as a fashion statement, by expressing our support for our favorite sports club, restaurant, or ideological cause.

Beyond any doubt, the best packaging *inside* a T-shirt is generally found in the Hooter's tee shirt, especially when worn by a Hooter's waitress. As the slogan says, it is truly "more than a mouthful."

Ippolito's, a restaurant on Holcomb Bridge Road just east of GA 400, also has a provocative T, encouraging its patrons to "EAT IT-alian."

An in-depth survey of what Atlanta-area residents are actually wearing, however, shows that the following are the 10 most popular T-shirts in the area:

1. The Braves—celebrating three straight National League West titles.
2. 1996 Olympics promotions.
3. The Falcons.
4. Tie—Georgia Tech & the University of Georgia.
6. Peachtree road race.
7. Life's A Peach.
8. The Hawks.
9. Coca-Cola.
10. Hard Rock Café Atlanta.

Indeed, almost every place in Atlanta has its own T-shirt, from the Martin Luther King Jr. Center to Six Flags Over Georgia.

In our opinion, however, none of these T-shirts lives up to the full marketing potential of Atlanta. We are therefore introducing a new T-shirt, soon to be on sale everywhere, to correct this deficiency: It is a T-shirt with a picture of our choice for mascot, appropriately titled:

"WHOGIVESADAMN."

It's the perfect clothing statement for every occasion. Be sure to buy one.

Heather

Leslie

Your Hand is in My Mouth!

Few things delight and challenge the imagination of children of all ages more than a puppet show. It is theatrical magic to take a few scraps of cloth that have been sewn together, shove your hand into them, and then proceed to tell a story. It doesn't really matter what the story is—it can be one the audience has heard a hundred times. It is the interaction of the puppets that charms and entertains, rather than the great drama.

Mad Hatter and friends rehearse for Alice

One of the most special attractions that can be found in Atlanta is the Center for Puppetry Arts, which is located in an old school building on Spring Street in Midtown. The school has been magically transformed into four theaters, a museum, teaching rooms, and all the other facilities needed to support the ongoing puppet programs.

And ongoing they are—the Center presents a very full platter for the Atlanta community to feast upon each year. Three major shows are held each year in the main theater—during the day on weekdays and in the evening on weekends. The show set for Fall 1993 is Alice in Wonderland, with Alice being played by an actress and the rest of the cast being puppets. We happened to catch part of the staging and rehearsal of the Mad Hatter's tea party, and it promises to be an irresistable piece of theater.

Shows set for 1994 are Aladdin and Journey to the Bottom of the Sea. Each show runs about two months.

During the summer, the Center stages a six-week festival, bringing in regional and national companies to stage shows. Like the Center's own major shows, these are directed at family entertainment.

In addition, the Center has a strong commitment to fostering adult puppet programming, and sponsors five innovative shows a year in what it calls its New Directions series. Shows set for the 1993-94 season include love stories, myths, and even some erotica. Many stretch the limits of puppetry and find ways to combine them with other media.

In addition, there are shorter, one-person programs being produced throughout the year, to showcase emerging puppeteers.

But performance is not the only dimension to

Peter Rabbit appeals to little children; dozing puppets await another turn in the limelight

A workshop in making puppets; one of theaters in the Museum

puppetry at the Center. There is also an outstanding collection of puppets, marionettes, and theaters in the Center's Puppetry Museum.

There is a lot of competition, but this may well be the best museum in Atlanta. It is not just a bunch of used puppets thrown into a few display cases. It is a thorough exploration of the development and history of the art of puppetry.

From Pigs in Space

There are, for instance, examples of puppet theaters from China, Japan, and other Far Eastern countries, as well as the puppets that would have been used in them. There are originals from the Punch and Judy tradition in England.

The Museum itself challenges the imagination. One of the real treasures of the display is a brick adorned in a short skirt, the kind ballet dancers wear. This brick was used, paradoxically enough, to portray a dancer in a puppet show many years ago in New York. When the puppeteer wanted to show one puppet standing on another's shoulders, he would just add another brick!

A Chinese puppet stage

One of the originals used by Waylon for his inspired "Madame" character is on display, as is numerous characters from the Jim Henson Muppet workshop, most notably the Captain and first mate from "Pigs in Space," which ran on the Electric Company two decades ago.

The museum also contains an area where kids can become their own puppeteers.

Behind the scenes, the Center also has full production facilities for creating puppets, building sets, and rehearsing. In one erstwhile classroom, puppets hang from the ceiling and are propped up along the walls, anticipating a time when they can be used again. It is an awesome display of sleeping creativity, waiting for some handsome prince puppeteer to come along and pluck them back into action again.

The Center also involves itself in teaching the arts it strives so well to preserve. Regular classes in making puppets, handling puppets, and developing skits and plays are taught at the Center.

The Center of Puppetry Arts brings to Atlanta a commitment to creativity and entertainment that is hard to find in most other cities. The programs they produce are of the highest professional level; the services they perform for the benefit of the community are extensive. As a nonprofit operation, the Center depends not only on its ticket sales but on the generosity of the community to prosper.

This is the kind of exciting program that deserves full and rich support from everyone, both in terms of attending its productions and in terms of supporting it financially. For information, call 873-3089.

The Abbey

Everyone who enjoys good food and wine should be grateful for European monasteries and abbeys, for out of the cloistered gates have come some of the greatest gastronomic developments. Dom Perignon, for instance, was a blind monk who developed an extraordinary genius for making wine. It was he who discovered the unique process of making champagne.

All of which is odd, because monasteries were originally established by ascetic monks who retreated to the deserts of Egypt to live a life of denial.

This spirit of denial may still persist at some monasteries, but not at The Abbey, a Midtown Atlanta restaurant that joyfully leads its patrons into indulgence—and first-class indulgence at that.

This magnificent establishment is located in a former Methodist Episcopal church at the corners of Ponce de Leon and Piedmont. All of the grandeur of the church—and more—has been left in tact—the vaulted ceilings, the stained glass windows, the organ loft, and the pulpit. Only the pews have been removed, to make way for tables.

A harpist plays lilting melodies from the loft. The waiters are dressed in the brown robes of monks. It is a wonderful atmosphere in which to enjoy an evening meal.

And the food lives up to the atmosphere. The menu is a combination of classic Continental and modern American. Instead of French onion soup, for instance, a Vidalia onion soup is offered—with a sweetbread crouton. It was superb. Also top notch was the black bean soup.

All of the entrées at The Abbey are works of art. We ordered the yellowfin tuna, roast pork tenderloin, hot smoked salmon, and free range chicken. The tuna was a huge yellowfin steak that was encrusted with almonds and macadamia nuts, then topped with shrimp and pineapple. The result was an excellent blend of texture and taste.

We also tried the hot smoked salmon, which was prepared with an oyster mushroom sauce. It turned out to be one of those special dishes that are so wonderful, you will never forget it.

Two of our party tried the roasted pork tenderloin, which was garnished with several jumbo shrimp wrapped in apple-smoked bacon and served with an habanero sauce. It was excellent. The final choice was the chicken, which came with garlic mashed potatoes and snow pea shoots. "Free range" refers to the fact that the chickens were not raised in cramped quarters, as is often the case. They are left to wander as they will. The result is far more flavorful than the usual.

Dessert was a many splendored thing—cheesecake in filo with fresh berries, chocolate carrot cake, a mango and chocolate macadamia nut pie, a black and white ganache with raspberry sauce, and a dish of fresh berries with creme anglaise. They all tasted divine, as well they should.

PART ONE

In the waning moments of the summer games in Barcleona, we were introduced to a new Olympic mascot...

The mascot who would represent Atlanta to the world in 1996...

Whatizit?

Whatizit, indeed! A grape?

a spermatozoa who had lost his way?

the butt of off-color jokes?

Kudzu Undercover saw the need for an in-depth investigation into this little blue thing and his past...

We found his family tree—it had been chopped down to make way for the new Olympic venues. It was now just a faggot.

(Look it up in your Funk & Wagnalls.)

And, of course, a long, lost half-brother...

Whogivesadamn

PART TWO

As we got to know him, we began to think Whogivesadamn might be a better choice for mascot than his brother. Compare...

Whatizit is blue.

Whogivesadamn is peach...

Georgia Peach!

Whatizit is confused; he expected you to name him.

And now that you have, he's still confused. Izzy? Is he—or isn't he?

Whogivesadamn knows who he is.

He just doesn't care!

Whatizit has spent most of the last year signing lucrative promotional contracts.

Whogivesadamn spent most of last year drinking beer.

Whatizit has denied his past.

Which, according to our unimpeachable source, is not as squeaky clean as you might think.

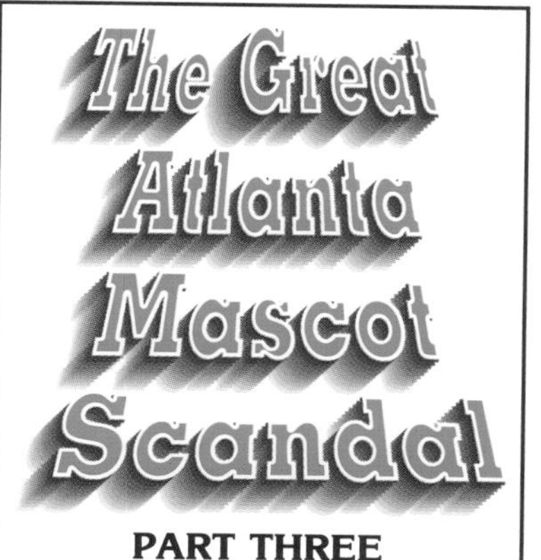

PART THREE

Whogivesadamn sat quietly, composing himself. Then he revealed the truth about Whatizit!

He posed for a while as Charlie Tuna...

Until he was exposed as an imposter....

With no taste at all!

He is not actually blue! His natural slimy green skin turned blue as a result of too much liposuction!

Whatizit can't spell.

He spent a term on City Council and no one even noticed...

Until he was caught accepting bribes.

He's actually an escaped specimen from the Center for Disease Control!

A virus that carries the dreaded bluebonnet plague...

which induces an unnatural craving for oleo instead of butter!

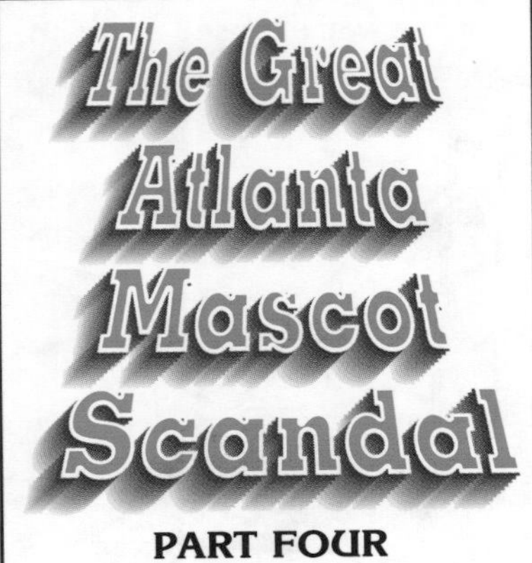

PART FOUR

The bluebonnet plague is a little known remnant that survived the bubonic plague.

People infected by it lose their sense of humor.

It makes you think you are cute when you are not.

It bores everyone to death...

Until they become Al Gore lookalikes!

Do you want Atlanta to catch the fever?

The Super Bowl won't be super unless it's fun!

No one will come to the Olympics if they think Atlanta has bad taste!

There's just one known antidote to the bluebonnet curse...

Whogivesadamn!

PART FIVE

So, let's give the mascot back to the people!

Hang Whatizit in effigy! Burn your Whatizit T-shirts!

And adopt Whogivesadamn as our unofficial mascot!

Whogivesadamn would be perfect leading the Tomahawk chant...

Hanging ten on the Wave...

Not *that* wave!

Opening used truck dealerships...

Inaugurating new show bars...

Lighting the Torch.

Whaddya say, Atlanta?

Whogivesadamn!

PART SIX

Famous folks who would endorse Whogivesadamn, if they could...

Rhett Butler...

Frankly, my dear...

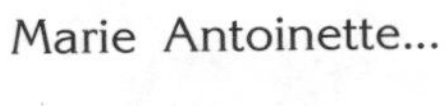

Marie Antoinette...

Let 'em eat cake.

Asa Candler...

Let 'em drink Coke.

W.C. Fields...

On the whole, I'd rather be in Philadelphia...

W.T. Sherman...

Just think of it as urban renewal...

P.T. Barnum.

There's a sucker born every minute.

A. Lincoln.

You can fool some of the people some of the time...

President Clinton.

But Hilary wouldn't let him.

PART SEVEN

Whogivesadamn is ready to serve as Atlanta's mascot!

Attracting new industry, creating new jobs!

Telling our kids to just say No!

Teaching Jane Fonda the real meaning of aerobics!

Giving Jerry Glanville a winning wardrobe...

Wiping out the deficit without raising taxes or cutting benefits!

Actually, he doesn't intend to do any of these things...

...after all, he doesn't really give a damn!

But if politicians can promise all this stuff and then do nothing at all, why can't he?

PART EIGHT

Atlanta can use Whogivesadamn's unique talents in many ways.

We can blow him up real big and use him as a blimp at the Super Bowl...

...unless, of course, Roseanne Arnold feels insulted!

He can become a news analyst for CNN...

He can win a pro-wrestling grudge match with those cartoon dots from 7-Up...

...and earn a multi-million dollar contract from Coca-Cola!

He could even teach the world to sing...

...That's *sing,* not *singe!*

He can be our city's most famous fictional character since Scarlett!

...except, of course, for Ted Turner.

Whogivesadamn is the future of Atlanta!

Someday, he may even end up on Stone Mountain!

So, don't ask what he can do for Atlanta...

...ask what you can do for Whogivesadamn!

The Fabulous Fox

Back in the late 20's, the Shriners decided to build a new temple in Midtown. As befits their tradition, they chose to build it in high Egyptian style, complete with onion domes and minarets. It was to be called the Yaarab Temple Shrine Mosque.

The stage of the Egyptian ballroom

Construction of such an elaborate facility soon became too costly, so the Shriners approached movie theater magnate William Fox. He took over part of the project, and between Fox and the Shriners, the building was completed. Fox ended up with a splendid movie theater capable of seating 4,000 patrons in opulent glory. Moviegoers entered the theater from Peachtree Street.

The Shriners ended up with several large meeting rooms, kitchen facilities, and other quarters that they needed for their functions. They entered through an elaborate doorway on Ponce de Leon.

There were also a variety of stores and cafés lining both Ponce de Leon and Peachtree. Only a restaurant remains.

Unfortunately, the temple/theater was opened just in time for the Great Depression—and bankruptcy. It prospered in the 40's, but as the population shifted outside the Perimeter, in the 50's and 60's, the Fox fell on hard times. It was bought by Southern Bell and scheduled for demolition, to make way for new offices, when a group of citizens became alarmed that Atlanta was about to lose a true architectural treasure. A nonprofit group was formed to buy the theater from Southern Bell and restore it.

Restoration is an ongoing task, but the Fox has now been back in operation since 1975. In addition to showing a regular schedule of movies, it rents out its stage for rock concerts, Broadway musicals, and other live performances.

With two grand ballrooms and full kitchen facilities, the Fox has also become a major venue for meetings, social events, and small conventions.

This is a remarkable building. Tours are conducted regularly, but the best way to discover the Fox is to attend one of the events. This is not a museum, where everything is roped off; it is a theater, where everything—including itself—is shown off. This philosophy extends even to the lavatories, which are appointed in the same high style as the rest of the building.

For information on tours, call 881-2100.

The entrance on Peachtree; one of several fountains; and a chair in the ladies' lounge

Run it up the Flagpole

Throughout the world, people argue about the silliest things. Here in Atlanta, for instance, there is currently a Big Stink (B.S.) about the state flag.

The original state flag featured the seal of Georgia against a blue background. Over the years, it has undergone many changes, as the state legislature toyed with it to avoid more serious issues. During the Civil Rights struggles of the 1950's, the flag was modified by the addition of a portion of a Confederate battle flag to the right of the seal, as a protest against Federal interference in state matters. This flag has remained the state flag since then.

With the Olympics approaching, the custodians of Georgia's image have decided it would be embarrassing to have all those athletes competing under the auspices of a Confederate battle flag. They gained support from area Civil Rights leaders, who declared the flag to be offensive. But when steps were taken to change the flag, all hell broke loose. Even in the New South, you do not mess with symbols of the Civil War without riling up a lot of people. Judging from the number of battle flags that have recently been affixed to pickup trucks, these folks take the threat to their flag seriously.

Ironically, the 1911 flag that the current one replaced—the one progressive thinkers want to re-turn to—is based on far more Con-federate symbolism than the one that so offends them. Facts, however, are usually unimportant in debates of this ilk.

At present, the issue remains a stalemate. Some people have suggested having two official Georgia state flags. This, however, seems like an unlikely solution.

1789

1870

1911

1956

The better choice, perhaps, would be to ditch both flags and start all over again. The state could hold a "Betsy Ross" contest, encouraging seamstresses from all over the state to submit designs for a new flag.

One obvious choice would be a simple blue banner with a Georgia peach smack in the center. Unfortunately, it would also tend to attract such snide remarks as: "Georgia—It's the Pits" or cartoons of the peach with a worm in it.

Our choice would be to keep the flag as it is but to require the planting of a single strand of kudzu at the base of each flagpole. Soon, the entire pole and flag would be covered by the creeping plant, and nothing would be visible but kudzu, blowing in the breeze.

If that idea is not a winner, then how about a flag bearing our choice for Atlanta mascot, Whogivesadamn. We believe he represents the attitude of most Georgians on this particular issue; we would also love to get the royalties from licensing his cute little peach face for thousands of flags to fly throughout Georgia.

Of course, we recognize that we might have to make some compromises in order to gain acceptance. We are perfectly willing, for example, to have the little fellow holding up a bottle of Coca-Cola. The banner could then read, "Always Georgia."

Isn't that the American Way?

Let's run it up the flagpole, and see who salutes.

Callaway Gardens

Some of humanity's greatest works of art cannot be found hanging in a gallery or museum, nor in the home of private collectors. For these are living works of art, that would die if moved indoors. They are the masterpieces of art we call the great gardens of the world.

The rare azalea

Georgia is fortunate enough to be the site of one of these gardens—Callaway Gardens—and Atlanta is blessed because it lies just one hour to its south.

The Callaways made a fortune in textiles in LaGrange, Georgia. They often took excursions to nearby Pine Mountain for relaxation. One day in 1930, Cason Callaway found a bright red, wild azalea that he knew he had never seen before. In fact, the species is so rare that it is native only to the area surrounding Pine Mountain.

The discovery of this rare flower inspired Cason to buy 2,500 acres of land in the area, for use as a weekend retreat. His holdings in the area eventually grew to 40,000 acres. Much of it was land that had been depleted by intensive cotton growing in earlier generations. At first, he tried to use modern agricultural techniques to restore the land and grow crops. But a massive flood ruined his dreams and left him knee deep in mud.

Once again, he was inspired. He abandoned the notion of farming, and shifted instead to developing the land into a thing of beauty—a lush garden that would be a tribute to what nature and man can accomplish together.

Cason built lakes, laid out a golf course, planted 700 varieties of azaleas, and gradually shaped the land into a paradise. At first, the retreat was only opened to Cason's best friends. But as his dream took shape, he was inspired once more—to open his paradise for all. This occurred in 1952, and in the 40 years since, Callaway Gardens has become world famous. And for good reason. Callaway Gardens is a real treasure—a masterpiece which changes and grows every year.

There are actually two parts to Callaway Gardens. The first is the garden itself, which consists of 7.5 miles of paved roads throughout the forest, with stops along the way at the lakes, the Ida Cason Callaway Memorial Chapel, the John A. Sibley Horticultural Center, the Cecil B. Day Butterfly Center, the Vegetable Garden, and a beach. The second is the Callaway Gardens Resort, a modern hotel and restaurant which attracts conferences, small conventions, and folks on vacation. It offers tennis, swimming, 63 holes of excellent golf, and seven dining facilities. Guests who wish to vacation at Callaway Gardens can stay either at the lodge or at guest cabins.

The Gardens are run by a nonprofit organization Cason created when he opened the gardens to the public. The Resort is operated as a business, but all profits go to support the nonprofit gardens.

Every facet of the Callaway complex is expertly run. One of the best times of the year to come visit is in the early spring, when the azaleas along the Azalea Trail are in bloom, but there is truly no "off" season at Callaway. Something fascinating is

Topiary critters—a snake, a fox, and a ram.

Flowers burst forth in the stained glass (left) of the Ida Cason Callaway Memorial Chapel

going on at all times, even Christmas. A light display called "Fantasy in Lights" made its debut in 1992 and became an instant hit. Thousands of cars lined up every night to drive along a 2.2-mile stretch of the gardens that had been lit up as a winter wonderland. The exhibit has been expanded for 1993 and has become a permanent part of the garden's programs.

It is this high caliber of imagination that distinguishes Callaway from other gardens or preserves. The displays here demonstrate how human inspiration and perspiration can subtly complement the inherent beauty of nature. Each year, for example, the garden creates an elaborate topiary display at the John A. Sibley Horticultural Center. This year, the theme of the display was wild animals. As you walked throughout the 5 acres of gardens at the Sibley Center, each bend or nook would produce a new surprise—a topiary sculpture of an animal—a snake hanging from a trellis, a hawk guarding its babies from a perch 20 feet away, possums hanging by their tails from a tree limb—even an alligator slithering into a pond! The whimsey of the topiary struck a perfect counterpoint to the resplendent beauty of the gardens.

A butterfly alights on a girl's finger

One part of the property is set aside for a garden of a different kind—a huge vegetable garden. This was the last major project initiated by Cason himself. Begun in 1960, the intent of the garden is to demonstrate scientific and practical applications of fruit and vegetable culture. More than 400 varieties of crops are grown there annually.

In essence, this garden within a garden is the culmination of Cason's original dream—the one that ended in knee-deep mud. Since 1984, it has been featured weekly on the PBS show "Victory Garden," as its Victory Garden South.

Quite possibly the most fascinating of all the major displays, however, is the Cecil B. Day Butterfly Center. Outdoor butterfly gardens are common throughout the South—in fact, there is a large one incorporated in the center. But indoor conservatories for butterflies are less common. Having seen a number in Europe, and having been impressed how much they fascinated both children and adults, Mrs. D.D. Smith offered to give the money to build such a conservatory in honor of her late husband, the founder of Days Inns.

She was not wrong. Even on a slow day, the

The beach

Cabins in the woods

Butterfly Center is an instant hit with almost everyone who visits it—but children especially. The conservatory is home for plants and butterflies native to Central and South America and Asia.

As wonderful as the major displays are, the real charm of Callaway Gardens lies in the miles and miles of woods, lakes, and wilderness in between these displays. One of the best ways to explore it is to rent a bike and pedal the 7.5 miles of the Discovery Bike Trail. It is much easier to absorb the spirit of the place by bicycle than by automobile.

One of the highlights of any visit to the gardens, for instance, should be a visit to the chapel Cason built in memory of his mother. Nestled by a small waterfall, the chapel is an excellent place for quiet reflection and meditation on the beauty and glory all around us, in nature. Consecrated by Dr. Norman Vincent Peale, the Ida Cason Callaway chapel is a thing of beauty itself. Even the stained glass designs remind us of the presence of divinity in nature.

It is clear that Cason had a mystical side to his nature, even though a successful businessman. He felt that it was God who was speaking to him as he stood knee-deep in mud, and although he was perhaps not exactly sure of the message, it is clear from the result that he was able to understand at some level, and put it into practice.

In talking about the gardens, Cason Callaway remarked, "Every child ought to see something beautiful before he's six years old—something he will remember all his life." His legacy makes it clear that Cason not only loved nature but also appreciated how the language of natural and divine beauty can speak to us all, especially to children.

Callaway Gardens does a magnificent job of giving people from all over the South, the nation, and the world the opportunity to see many beautiful things—any one of which could change their lives, if they would open their heart and respond to this beauty with the best within them. In the first 40 years the gardens have been opened to the public, more than 20 million people have visited Cason's dream. Each year, that number increases by almost one million more.

This is a wonderful example of what philanthropy ought to be. Only someone with great wealth could have created something this magnificent; only someone with great charity in his heart would give it to the public for their enjoyment and inspiration.

Callaway Gardens is located on U.S. Highway 27 in Pine Mountain. From Atlanta, take I-85 south to I-185; follow it to U.S. 27, which will lead you to both the resort and gardens.

And, oh yes—the rare azaleas now grow everywhere throughout the gardens. In fact, the flower design has been adopted as Callaway Garden's logo.

The beginning of one of many trails at Callaway.

The Trail of Tears

For most people, the history of Atlanta began with the start of construction on the Western & Atlantic railroad in 1837. In point of fact, however, the area had been a major intersection of Indian trails for years before. Both the Cherokee and Creek tribes used trails that converged on the Atlanta area, then crossed the Chattahoochee at convenient fords. Indeed, there was an Indian village called Standing Peachtree near the point where Peachtree Creek enters the Chattahoochee.

Recent archaeological discoveries indicate that the Cherokees had been thriving in this region—and all of north Georgia—for hundreds of years.

One of the major reasons why Atlanta could not be developed until the 1840's—despite the fact that Georgia was colonized in 1730—was that it was part of land owned by the Cherokee nation.

Sequoyah, a famous Cherokee

Among all of the American Indian tribes, the Cherokees made the greatest effort to cooperate with the white settlers and adapt their customs. They traded with the settlers and allowed the displaced Europeans to purchase the land that they needed for their settlements and expansion. As a result, there was only a minimum of strife and animosity between the natives and the settlers.

Perhaps the greatest mistake the Cherokees made was to side with the British during the War of Independence. Several initiatives led by the Cherokees against U.S. forces ended in complete humiliation of the Cherokees, who were forced to withdraw into neutrality and surrender lands. The Cherokee nation became concentrated in the Appalachian regions of the Carolinas and Georgia.

There they lived peaceably, trading with the white settlers—until gold was discovered in Dahlonega, in the heart of Cherokee lands. A campaign to uproot the Indians from their lands began almost immediately. Under a treaty that was signed by only a minority of the Cherokees, the nation agreed to cede to the U.S. title to all of their lands east of the Mississippi. In return, the Cherokee nation received compensation of $5 million.

The only available land for the Indians to be transported to was in Oklahoma. During the years 1838 and 1839, the Indians were forced to leave Georgia and their other eastern lands and move their communities to Oklahoma. En route, the tribe lost 4,000 of its 18,000 members to disease and the rigors of the journey. When they were finally resettled in Oklahoma, reprisals were made against many of the tribe members who had signed the fateful agreement, thus reducing their numbers even further.

Nonetheless, the Cherokee lived as a semi-autonomous nation in Oklahoma—along with four other tribes displaced from the Southeast—for 75 years, until Oklahoma was granted statehood. At that time, the tribal governments ceased to exist and the Indians became citizens of the U.S.

Three thousand Cherokees managed to escape deportation by hiding out in the Georgia mountains. Once the program of removal was completed, they quietly set up villages and continued to live—as residents of Georgia, not the Cherokee nation. The number of Cherokees residing in Georgia today is approximately 20,000—more than the number that was deported to Oklahoma 150 years ago.

Indian artifacts continue to be discovered throughout the north part of the state. As more and more archaeological finds are made, the likelihood increases that modern Atlanta will eventually give the Cherokee nation the honor and recognition that it deserves.

Without Standing Peachtree, after all, who can say where the railroad surveyor might have driven the fateful stake?

Atlanta Trivia Test

How much do you know about Atlanta? Here are a few questions which should test your knowledge. Native Atlantans should know all of the answers. Transplants should score at least 80 percent. Visitors are not expected to know anything, as long as they are wearing a Whogivesadamn T-shirt.

1. The population of Atlanta is :
   a. Under 500,000.
   b. Between 500,000 and 1 million.
   c. Between 1 and 2 million.
   d. Between 2 and 3 million.
2. *Gone With the Wind* was filmed:
   a. In Atlanta.
   b. In Hollywood.
   c. At Tara.
   d. In Jonesboro.
3. During the Civil War, the city of Atlanta was burned by:
   a. Sherman's troops.
   b. Confederate troops as they retreated.
   c. Residents who looted businesses during the Confederate Army's retreat.
   d. All of the above.
4. Lake Lanier is named after Sidney Lanier, who is famous for his work as a:
   a. Musician.
   b. Poet.
   c. Hydroplane pilot.
   d. Geologist.
5. According to the motto of the Atlanta *Journal*, it:
   a. Covers Dixie like the dew.
   b. Brings light into darkness.
   c. Awakens Atlanta in the morning.
   d. Covers Dixie like kudzu.
6. Stone Mountain was originally called:
   a. Granite Mountain.
   b. Big Mountain.
   c. Rock Mountain.
   d. Big Rock Candy Mountain.
7. A geological oddity about Atlanta is that the Downtown is built on:
   a. A major seismic fault.
   b. The site of ancient underground springs, which cause sinkholes to emerge.
   c. Solid granite.
   d. The continental divide for the Eastern U.S.
8. The first year Coca-Cola was introduced, it turned a net profit of:
   a. $25,000.
   b. $7,500.
   c. $75.
   d. It lost $25.
9. Which Atlanta college was nicknamed "Coca-Cola U.," because of the large gifts which helped establish it?
   a. Emory.
   b. Georgia Tech.
   c. Georgia State.
   d. Atlanta University.
10. When the first train puffed into Atlanta in 1845 from Augusta, the 173-mile ride set a record for:
   a. The fastest trip in railroad history.
   b. The first trip on which food was served.
   c. The longest trip in railroad history.
   d. The most drunks who can be crammed into a caboose.
11. In early drafts of *Gone With the Wind,* Scarlett O'Hara was called:
   a. Maggie.
   b. Buttercup.
   c. Pansy.
   d. Petunia.

ANSWERS:

1. A. The population of metro Atlanta is almost 3 million, but the city of Atlanta has less than 400,000 residents.
2. B. Red clay had to be shipped to Hollywood and scattered on the set, to make it look like Georgia.
3. D. The most damage may have been done by retreating Confederate troops, when they blew up the ammunition dump.
4. B. You get extra credit if you can recite one of his poems—or even mention the title of one.
5. A. Could we have made this up?
6. C.
7. D.
8. D. Well, $24.96 to be exact.
9. A.
10. C.
11. C.

Always Coca-Cola

We are a world of many peoples, speaking many languages, believing many creeds, adhering to many customs, and often fighting among ourselves. But for all of the diversity to be found throughout the planet, there is one thing we all have in common: We all drink Coke.

And so when tourists from all over the world visit Atlanta, one of the first places they visit is The World of Coke, just between the Underground and the State Capitol.

The World of Coke, of course, is a blatant tribute to one of America's greatest business success stories. But since we all drink Coke, it is an irresistable exhibit—something between a shrine to modern marketing and a Disneyesque view of the world. It is one of the most popular exhibits in Atlanta.

Entrance to the World of Coke

To tour The World of Coke, you take an elevator to the top floor and then work your way down. The display tells the story of the development and marketing of Coke over the past 100 years, ever since Doc Pemberton, an Atlanta druggist, first concocted French wine cola, the predecessor of Coca-Cola.

When Coke first emerged, it was sold as a patent medicine—for headache relief! The syrup was to be mixed with tap water and then drunk. It was sold primarily to druggists, who then retailed it to customers in need of relief. One of these druggists accidentally mixed the syrup with soda instead of tap water one day, and the carbonated cola was invented. It proved so popular that everyone began mixing Coke with soda.

It is not the story of Coca-Cola that fascinates the crowds, though; it is the wealth of Coke paraphernalia from days gone by: billboards, coolers, even advertisements. In one display, you can listen to jingles from Coke commercials, as sung by some of the world's great singers. Or, you can find ads or displays you can remember from being a kid—when a Coke was 5 cents.

In addition to the nostalgia, there are also several high tech displays—a fantasy bottling operation and a neon dispenser which shoots the Coke product of your choice through the air, into your cup.

At the end of a tour, you can buy Coke T-shirts and other souvenirs in the gift shop.

A fantasy vision of the Coca-Cola bottling operation.

Woodruff Arts Center

Thirty years ago, more than 100 arts enthusiasts from Atlanta died in a plane crash at Orly Field in Paris. Stunned by this accident, the government of France decided to give to the people of Atlanta a bronze casting of Rodin's sculpture, The Shade, in memory of those who died. But this created a new dilemma—where to exhibit it?

The Shade

The answer came from Robert Woodruff, chairman of Coca-Cola, who stepped forward to finance construction of the Atlanta Memorial Arts Center—later renamed the Woodruff Arts Center.

Completed in 1968, the Woodruff is unique, in that it houses not one but three distinct arts organizations—four, if you count the High Museum next door, which now has its own building but shares the property. The other three are the Atlantic Symphony Orchestra, the Alliance Theater Company, and the Atlanta College of Art.

The Woodruff is an impressive concept, but after 25 years it is slowly becoming outdated. As each of the groups served by the Woodruff has grown, they have gradually outstripped the capacity of the center to fulfill their needs. The symphony, for example, is rapidly gaining a reputation under conductor Yoel Levi as being one of the best orchestras in the world. But the better the symphony becomes, the more blatant the lack of first-class acoustics becomes as well.

The Woodruff Center is the focus for the classical performing arts in Atlanta, but it does not actually produce or stage anything. That function is left to its member groups, which develop their own schedules, based on their own visions.

Under Levi, the vision guiding the symphony seems to be clear and bright. It is always expensive to support 100 gifted musicians, but in this case, the reward to the community is clearly worthwhile.

The clarity of vision at the Alliance is less certain. It has been showered with praise for its performances of avant-garde theater—but declining ticket sales indicate that public tastes may not concur.

The Cultural Olympiad which will be staged in harmony with the 1996 Olympic Games will give the Woodruff consortium a new opportunity to refine and re-energize their artistic visions.

The main hall at the Woodruff Center; outside, a statue in honor of Robert Woodruff

Bulloch Hall

The fireplace in one of the formal rooms; Bulloch Hall in its full glory

By the time the legendary stake was driven into the ground marking the terminal of the Western and Atlantic Railroad—and the beginning of Atlanta—Roswell was already a thriving community 30 miles to the north. It was founded by Roswell King shortly after the gold rush in Dahlonega began to die down. King had noted that Roswell would be an ideal location to build a mill—which he did. Soon Roswell was a prosperous textile town.

One of King's partners in the mill was James Bulloch, who built the grand Bulloch Hall in 1840, one of the best examples of the true temple style of Greek Revival architecture anywhere in the South. Other leading Roswellians also built homes—and a church—at the same time, making Magnolia Street in Roswell a very special place.

In Bulloch Hall, the mother of Teddy Roosevelt and the grandmother of Eleanor Roosevelt—Mittie Bulloch—was born and married.

Now owned by the city, tours can be arranged by calling in advance. The hall is used for classes in Southern crafts such as cooking, quilt-ing, and so on. From time to time, the hall also sponsors evenings of storytelling.

Bulloch Hall is located 1 block west of the historic town square, which is at the junction of Roswell Road to Marietta and Atlanta Highway. The telephone is 992-1731.

Cooking was done on an open fire in the kitchen; Teddy Roosevelt visits Bulloch Hall in 1905.

GWTW Blows Atlanta Away

Margaret Mitchell's blockbuster novel, *Gone With the Wind,* became a runaway bestseller when it was published in 1936. Three years later, as the headline below attests, the movie version of the book made its debut to great hoopla in Atlanta.

The movie may have been more destructive to Atlanta than all of Sherman's army.

This is not to imply that it is not a great movie, one of the great romantic stories of all time. But it has presented to the world a distorted view of the Civil War, the South, and Atlanta.

Folks who know nothing about Atlanta except what they have seen on the silver screen come to visit the city. They want to know: "Where is Tara?" "Where are Rhett and Scarlett buried?"

There is no Tara—there never was a Tara. It is a fictional place created out of the author's imagination. And actually, no place like the movie's Tara ever existed anywhere close to Atlanta. That style of plantation mansion was found on the coast. Plantation homes around Atlanta were far more modest. And plantation life was completely different than that portrayed.

Rhett and Scarlet, being fictional characters, are not buried anywhere.

Margaret Mitchell hated the movie. She felt that it failed to capture the heart and soul of the book, simplifying a complex tale into a sentimental tear jerker.

The Atlanta History Center labors hard to correct the misinformation spread by the movie— yet the movie has become so closely identified with Atlanta that the history center feels compelled to feature an entire display on the filming of *Gone With the Wind.* Think of the paradox—a movie treated like a central part of a city's history and heritage. It's not because the history center wants it that way; it's because tourists and visitors want Atlanta to uphold the images in the movie. They want fantasy and illusion, not history.

The history of Atlanta is rich enough that it does not have to be woven out of dining room curtains.

The Weather
Yesterday: High, 50. Low, 29.
Today: Fair, Warmer. Low, 26.

THE ATLANTA CONSTITUTION

The Constitution Leads in City Home Delivered, Total City and Trading Territory Circulation

The South's Standard Newspaper

VOL. LXXII, No. 176. ATLANTA, GA., FRIDAY MORNING, DECEMBER

RHETT BUTLER AT FIVE POINTS

Hedgerose Heights Inn

Back in the first half of this century, an enterprising land developer proposed a new subdivision in Buckhead. He called it "Hedgerose Heights," although there is no indication that there was a single hedgerose in the area at the time.

The area has been built up for years, but no one calls it Hedgerose Heights anymore. The residences that were built by the developer have largely become quaint shops, salons, offices, and restaurants.

The one-time residence that houses the Hedgerose Heights Inn was an antique store prior to its incarnation as a restaurant. During remodeling, an old plat for the subdivision was uncovered. It has been framed and hangs in the bar. And the restaurant assumed the name, preserving it for at least another chunk of posterity.

Penny & Heinz Schwab

If all goes well, the name Hedgerose Heights will be around a long time. In the 12 years since it opened, it has become one of the finest formal restaurants in town. In our opinion, it may well be number one.

Although small—maximum seating is 60—the dining room is both comfortable and elegant at the same time. Few places in town have been appointed in such an exquisite style, right down to the choice of linen, silverware, and dishes.

But the food, of course, is the star. Each meal begins with a small appetizer, compliments of the chef, Heinz Schwab. The evening we dined there, it was strips of duck served with a raspberry confit. It was a refreshing way to begin.

Everything that followed was equally first-rate. A bowl of chilled cream of asparagus with crabmeat soup was one of the finest we've ever tasted. The Stromboli salad was a marvelous treatment of tomatoes, oranges, and onion. The Swiss salad is a plate of seven different prepared salads, each outstanding.

Dinner entrées were Dover sole served with purple potatoes—the sole melted deliciously in your mouth—and buffalo steak served with a black bean salsa and sweet potato straws. The meat was tender and the salsa had a wonderful kick to it.

For dessert, we tried the black currant soufflé and a Swiss creme brulée. The soufflé was served with a slab of chocolate and whipped cream on top. As you broke the top, the chocolate and cream sank down and mixed with the currant filling, producing a truly superb flavor. The creme brulée was everything that dish should be.

All of this was served with style and panache. Hedgerose Heights Inn is expensive—two people can expect to spend $90 or more—but if your budget allows, it is certainly worth it.

Call 233-7673 for reservations.

Breathing Life into History

When kids go on vacation they want to go to Six Flags or the beach. Parents usually want to make the vacation a learning experience, so they insist on visiting every museum and cultural shrine along the way. The kids, who have already had enough history in school, feel as though they are getting another dose forced down their throats.

The Swan House

The Atlanta History Center proves that history does not have to be dry and boring. It can be just as exciting and energizing as a trip to an amusement park. That is quite an achievement.

The history center is blessed with a first-rate location and setting, a 32-acre parcel of land just one block west of Peachtree Street on West Paces Ferry Road, in the heart of Buckhead. The land was formerly the estate of the Edward Inman family, and the baronial mansion Inman built for his wife and himself remains as a central attraction at the center.

The mansion is known as the Swan House. Mrs. Inman loved swans, and so decorative swans appear, in one way or another, in every room of the house. After she died, the property was acquired by the history center, which maintains it and shows it to the public with regular daily tours.

The Swan House is not as overtly historic as, say, a Civil War battlefield, and that is a large part of its charm. It looks at the history of Atlanta from 1925 to 1965 through the eyes of one of its wealthiest families and how they lived. In its way, it is striking testament to the ability of Atlanta to survive and rebuild.

There are rooms in the Swan House that are so opulent that they will take your breath away. It is a truly fascinating glimpse at the way the very rich lived in the first part of this century.

Even more wonderful are the gardens and grounds around the mansion. Trails have been cut throughout the grounds, so that visitors can explore the estate at leisure. As you stroll along, you never know what you may encounter next—a waterfall, a stone elephant, or a Victorian playhouse.

Using this basic setting the history center has

The dining room at the Swan House; an elephant sculpture graces a garden path

A pleasant gazebo at the history center

One of a few cars ever built in Atlanta waits for the opening of the new building

gradually created a first-rate history complex. They acquired the buildings from one of the few "plantations" in the Atlanta area that was not destroyed by the Civil War, moved them here, and rebuilt them. The result is the Tullie Smith plantation.

For people who associate the word "plantation" with the name "Tara," this part of the complex will be an eye-opener. For this was a very humble plantation. The main house was a small, clapboard cottage, not a big mansion. The owners worked side by side in the cotton fields with the slaves.

It is not just the buildings that have been restored; the daily routine of the plantation has been as well. Goats and sheep are kept in a barn; next door, a blacksmith's forge is used daily to make tools and hardware. A smokehouse cures bacon slabs and ribs, and when the weather is temperate, meals are cooked daily in the kitchen. Having seen how the rich lived in Buckhead three generations ago, visitors can also see how the typical plantation was actually run 150 years ago.

There is even a small planting of cotton!

Until this year, the rest of the exhibits at the Atlanta History Center have been on display at McElreath Hall, which also serves as quarters for the center's staff and home for an extensive research library. The library will continue to operate out of McElreath Hall and is open to anyone wishing to research any subject of Atlanta's history.

The rest of the center, however, has just moved into a brand new, $11 million facility which will house the major exhibits of the center on the main floor and staff offices and support functions on the lower floor. The official dedication of the new building was October 23, 1993.

The lobby of the new facility has been built to

The new home for the Atlanta History Center

resemble a train station during the time when railroad was king.

The tour of the exhibits begins with a short film introducing visitors to Atlanta in general and the history center in specific. It then adjourns to the exhibits themselves.

There are five primary exhibits in the new center:

1. Metropolitan Frontiers, which contrasts the modern city of Atlanta with its rich heritage as a rural frontier town, a transportation center, a city of commerce, and a suburban metropolis. One of the most fascinating elements in this exhibit is the Shotgun House, an actual house that was saved from demolition, moved to the center, and completely rebuilt. Its name derives from the simplicity of its design, in that you can fire a shotgun through the front door and out the back door without striking any interior wall (or, we hope, occupants).

2. Gone for a Soldier, a small exhibit commemorating the Civil War.

3. The Herndon's, which will explore the development of the black upper class in Atlanta, focusing on the story of the wealthiest black family in Atlanta's history.

4. Handed On, a showcase of folk crafts and their importance in Southern life.

5. Days to Remember, an exhibit examining the traditional celebrations of Atlanta's ethnic communities throughout the year.

As with the exhibits outside the hall, the goal of these displays is not just to warehouse old artifacts. An imaginative and creative effort is made to breathe new life into the past, and show the debt of the modern city of Atlanta to its history. On the whole, the history center succeeds admirably well.

One of the most exciting features about the new center is the inclusion of 2,500 square feet of classrooms and discovery centers to make it easier for schoolchildren to take advantage of the many wonders at the center. In fact, they have their own special entrance.

The Atlanta History Center is located at 3101 Andrews Drive in the Buckhead section of Atlanta. It is easily reached by turning west on West Paces Ferry Road from Peachtree Street and traveling a couple of blocks to Andrews Drive. There is plenty of parking on the grounds. The center is open every day from 9 to 5:30, except on Sunday, when hours are noon to 5:30. Admission is $6 for adults, $4.50 for college students and senior citizens, and $3 for youth. Children under 6 are free. In addition, admission is free for all ages each Thursday afternoon from 1 to 5:30. Admission covers the cost of all tours and exhibits. Access to the library is free.

The Atlanta History Center plays an important role in defining the essence of this city.

An apprentice learns blacksmithing at Tullie Smith farm; a cottage at the farm

On the Wild Side

Once upon a time, when almost everyone in America grew up on a farm, or close to one, kids interacted with animals on a daily basis. Some were tame—barnyard animals—but just as many were not. Foxes, bears, deer, coyotes, and all manner of birds were common encounters of the average American child.

Not so in our urban society. For many kids growing up in America today, the zoo represents their only chance to see and interact with animals—and in most cases, these are animals from far, exotic shores, be it Africa, Asia, or South America, not the north Georgia woods.

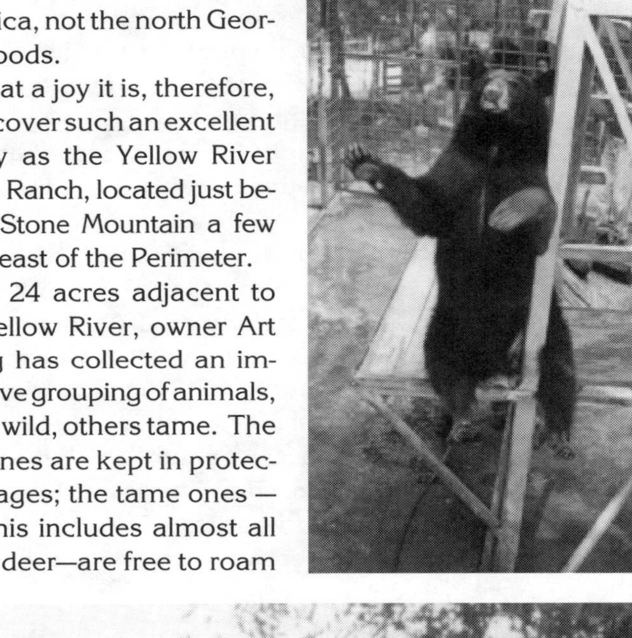

What a joy it is, therefore, to discover such an excellent facility as the Yellow River Game Ranch, located just beyond Stone Mountain a few miles east of the Perimeter.

On 24 acres adjacent to the Yellow River, owner Art Rilling has collected an impressive grouping of animals, some wild, others tame. The wild ones are kept in protective cages; the tame ones — and this includes almost all of his deer—are free to roam as they please. If they take a liking to you, they may even come nuzzle up and make your acquaintance.

A trail winds its way throughout the entire 24 acres. Each step along it brings you to another animal—another opportunity to explore and learn.

Each animal is treated according to its character. The deer, for example, are never caged up unless they are being treated medically. The black bears, on the other hand, are kept in a cage, but with plenty of opportunities to show off and ham it up. Like a dog, they love to beg for food from visitors. Rilling feeds the animals a balanced diet every day, yet still encourages visitors to interact with the animals by feeding them. The animals seem to enjoy the attention and interest as much as actually receiving the snacks.

There are more animals at the Yellow River Game Ranch than Noah ever imagined cramming into the ark. There are sheep, goats, geese, and ducks—but also hawks, mountain lions, peacocks, skunks, and bobcats.

A bear pretends he's a dog; a goat crosses the bridge; Art Rilling feeds a goat

A little dude finds out how easy it is to feed the deer; ducks play in a pond

Another animal that is willing to perform is the goat. Rilling has constructed an elaborate bridge that actually crosses the path about 20 feet up. Upon hearing a bell, a goat will rush up a long incline to a platform, run across the bridge, and end up on the platform on the other side of the path, where a treat awaits him.

Over the years, Rilling has been responsible for nursing back to health any number of deer and other animals that have been injured in accidents and left to die. He knows each animal on the ranch and its history, and understands animal psychology extremely well.

At the same time, he is a good promoter. He has named his one groundhog General Lee, and every February 2nd he invites folks to come out to the ranch to see if General Lee is predicting more winter or an early spring. In May, he holds a sheep shearing day. A professional sheep shearer comes in to relieve the sheep of their wool coats—but visitors to the park that day are invited to try their hands at sheep shearing, too.

During the fall, he stages hayrides after regular ranch hours, complete with hot dog roasts.

The promotions help get people to come to the ranch, but once they are there, curiosity takes over and holds their interest naturally. The place is an instant hit with children, who love being able to interact so closely with the animals.

Picnic grounds are provided for families that want to spend a whole day. The ranch is also a popular attraction for school field trips.

The Yellow River Game Ranch is located at 4525 U.S. Highway 78, just past the Yellow River, only a pebble's throw from Stone Mountain. In fact, it operated for a number of years in Stone Mountain Park, until moving to the Yellow River a number of years ago.

Fawns that have been rescued from the highway are nursed; a buck stops here

The Building of a Mall

An elevator "going up"

According to history, the first building erected in Atlanta was a trading post, to supply the needs of early settlers and the workers building the new railroad. Trading posts have long ago been supplanted by general stores; at the turn of the century, they were dwarfed by mammoth department stores. In the last half of this century, the emphasis has turned first to shopping centers and then, more recently, to shopping malls.

There are plenty of shopping malls around Atlanta, but none

The north entrance to the new Rich's at North Point Mall

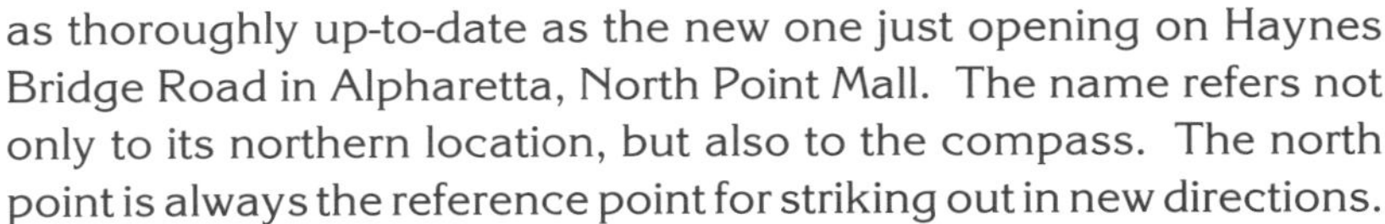

as thoroughly up-to-date as the new one just opening on Haynes Bridge Road in Alpharetta, North Point Mall. The name refers not only to its northern location, but also to the compass. The north point is always the reference point for striking out in new directions.

This mall is more than just a big warehouse for stores; it is, as they say in the computer world, user friendly. It is designed to be pleasant to visit, both on the outside and the inside. Outside, much of the architecture is striking, especially Rich's and the entranceways to the mall. Inside, the decor gives the mall a New Orleans-style flair. Even though it covers more than a million square feet, it is easy to get around and move from store to store.

There is even a carousel next to the fast food court to make the chore of shopping easier on little feet.

In addition to Rich's, the mall is anchored by Lord & Taylor, Sears, JCPenney, and Mervyn's, with room for a sixth anchor if that materializes. Smaller stores feature many of the usual outlets found at malls, plus a few additions: Perfumania; The Ozone, an electronics store owned by Braves' star Otis Nixon; This End Up, a furniture store; Azhar's Oriental Rugs; The Disney Store; The Great Train Store; and Maison du Popcorn.

Mick's will anchor the restaurant scene, and a well-rounded food court will feature everything from cajun cuisine to Chinese. Haagen Dazs will be on hand to take care of any ice cream deficiencies.

North Point is located just east of Georgia 400 at the Haynes Bridge exit. Directly to the south and east of the mall, two strip shopping centers are being built, featuring a Barnes and Noble, an Office Max, and a number of new restaurants. When finished, it will be possible to shop continuously from Haynes Bridge Road to Mansell Road, then get back on Georgia 400 and drive home.

The North will be buying at North Point.

Kudzu Café

Kudzu, it turns out, is a great marketing tool. The Kudzu Café, for instance, had a billboard a while back that proclaimed "they were taking over Buckhead." The irresistible growth of kudzu is a metaphor some folks just can't refrain from capitalizing on.

It also turns out that kudzu, when mashed, dried, and ground into a floury substance by Zen monks who obviously have nothing better to do, is edible. In fact, it is highly prized among the Japanese and commands an extravagant price in that fair land, probably along the order of saffron.

Our investigative team did not discover whether or not the proprietors of the Kudzu Café knew all this about kudzu before they chose this particular name—or if they were just having fun. We hope it is the latter, and that they are not really vegetarian kamikazes here to foist tofu and kudzu upon unsuspecting diners. Fortunately, there is no sign of this being true, except for the one ominous note that their salads are topped with a secret Kudzu recipe. Is that a secret recipe of Kudzu Café—or a secret recipe made with kudzu? Only the Kudzu knows.

Even without mysteries such as these, the Kudzu Café is a delightful place to dine—and uncontestably one of the hottest places to eat, either in Buckhead or anywhere in town. The best way to describe their cuisine is to imagine a head-on crash between Southern cooking and nouvelle cuisine. The Kudzu menu would be the result.

There are, for example, such undisputably Southern items on the menu as hush puppies, Savannah crab cakes, barbequed chicken, roasted chicken, meat loaf, grilled corn on the cob, and fried green tomatoes. You can also order a vegetable plate, which is a page torn directly out of Southern cooking.

On the other hand, the above mentioned roasted chicken is served with a red pepper jelly which makes it much more exciting than chicken has any right to be—but not classic Southern.

In fact, the chef manages to put his own imprimatur on just about every dish offered. The spaghetti and meat sauce is a wonderfully bold interpretation of an old cliché, but if you are expecting the old cliché, you will be in for the surprise of your life.

Another outstanding entrée is the hickory grilled smoked pork chop, which is served with a zesty applesauce.

The entrées are served with a choice of two side dishes: mashed potatoes, french fries, apple cider slaw, grilled corn on the cob, sautéed spinach, or snap peas. You can also order Brussels sprouts.

Desserts run the gamut from ice cream and shakes to hot pecan pie and hot peach bread pudding.

The restaurant is very large and always packed. It is tastefully decorated in kudzu green—in fact, the spirit of kudzu is very nicely integrated throughout the whole restaurant. The service is friendly, prompt, helpful, and courteous.

Kudzu Café is located at 3215 Peachtree Road in Buckhead, just a couple of blocks south of Lenox Mall. In addition to dinner, lunch is served daily. Brunch is served Saturday and Sunday from 11 to 2:30. Prices are moderate at dinner but a little pricey at lunch.

Famous Transplants

Just 155 years ago, the city of Atlanta did not exist. It was largely destroyed during the Civil War, but rebuilt to become a great city. In 1917, a large portion of Downtown was ravaged by fire. Once again Atlanta rebuilt.

Many native sons and daughters have been instrumental in building Atlanta—but it has also benefitted greatly from the skill and labor of "transplants"—the local label for folks who have moved here from elsewhere in the country.

Actually, with the rapid growth of Atlanta in recent decades, there must be more transplants in the population than native Atlantans. Some of the key transplants throughout Atlanta's history have been:

Thomson

Roswell King, a coastal land agent, was sent by his company to keep tabs on the gold rush in Dahlonega. On various side trips, he became familiar with the land north of Atlanta. As the gold fever subsided, he purchased a large parcel of land along Vickery Creek, built a mill, and founded the town of Roswell. It was already prospering by the time Atlanta was founded.

Morris Reich grew up in Hungary, emigrating to the United States as a boy. He was only 20 when he opened a dry goods store on Whitehall Street in Atlanta. He called it Rich's, and thus one of the greatest department store chains of the South was founded.

Hannibal Kimball, a native of Maine, came to Atlanta as an agent of the Pullman Company. He ended up in charge of the first Cotton States Exposition, which was held in 1881 and was a huge success.

Born in Ohio, **John Heisman** came to Atlanta to coach the Georgia Tech football team. It was under his tenure that Georgia Tech set the all-time record for most points scored in a game by beating Cumberland University 222-0—in a game that was called with seven minutes to go because of the magnitude of the rout. The Heisman Trophy, which is given each year to the outstanding college football player, is named in his honor.

Lemuel Grant, a native of Maine, had also come to Georgia to work on the railroad, as chief engineer. During the war, he stayed in Atlanta. In 1863, he was commissioned to fortify the city of Atlanta against possible attack from the North. With slave labor hired from nearby plantations, he dug trenches and erected 12-foot palisades. In all, the defenseworks encircled the entire city at a distance of two miles from the heart of town. It was a stout defense, but in the end, not enough.

Grant

Grant Park, which houses Zoo Atlanta and the Cyclorama, is named for Lemuel Grant.

J. Edgar Thomson was born in Pennsylvania. He came to Georgia to build the first railroad into Atlanta, which was still known then as Marthasville. The first train into Marthasville arrived on September 15, 1845 from Augusta. It was also Thomson who changed the name of the railroad terminal to Atlanta, since Marthasville was too hard to handwrite. Within three months, the name of the city was legally changed as well.

C.E. Woolman, a native of Indiana, came to Georgia to help fight the boll weevil, which was threatening to wipe out cotton production. It was his idea to spray the cotton crops with pesticides from the air. Thus was crop dusting born. He formed a small fleet of airplanes to dust crops and transport mail—a company that later grew into Delta Airlines, which has been headquartered in Atlanta since 1941.

Henry Aaron, who grew up in Mobile, Alabama, came to Atlanta when the Braves baseball team moved here from Milwaukee in 1966. He set the world on its ear on April 9, 1974, when he cracked his 715th major league home run in a game against the Los Angeles Dodgers. This broke the legendary record of Babe Ruth and created a new legend. Hammerin' Hank continues to live in Atlanta, serving as vice-president of the Braves.

The Hall of Fame

As with any hall of fame, the danger of listing the most important Atlantans throughout the history of the city lies in omitting important ones. Nonetheless, any list of outstanding citizens from the past should definitely include:

Hardy Ivy, who was the first settler and major landowner in the Atlanta area. He bought more than 200 acres of what is now prime real estate in 1839. In light of the advent of kudzu 100 years later, one wonders if his name was prophetic.

James M. Calhoun, mayor of Atlanta who surrendered the city to Sherman after Confederate troops retreated.

Candler

Mitchell

Henry Grady was the dynamic editor of the Atlanta *Constitution* from 1880 to 1889, when he died. He was a leading advocate of the "New South," which included transforming the South from an agricultural to an industrial region—and normalizing race relations. In a speech in New York attended by William Sherman, he twitted the general about "having been kind of careless about fire," but added: "from the ashes we have raised a brave and beautiful city."

Herndon

John S. Pemberton was the developer of Coca-Cola in 1886. Within five years, he had sold out his interest in the soft drink for $2,300 to **Asa G. Candler.** It was Candler who turned Coke into a carbonated beverage and supervised the creation of one of the most massive distribution systems in the world. After World War I, he sold out for $25 million and devoted the rest of his life to philanthropy.

Robert Woodruff was the son of one of the investors who bought Coca-Cola, and took over running the company four years after the purchase. He ran the company for 60 years, building it into the dominant business that it is. He also became a major philanthropist, giving at least $250 million to charitable causes and foundations.

Joel Chandler Harris took over as editor of the *Constitution* following Grady's death, but gained international fame as author of the Uncle Remus stories.

Alonzo Herndon, a freed slave, worked his way up from field laborer to become the wealthiest black man in America—and a major philanthropist of black causes. His son **Norris** continued the tradition of philanthropy, giving the Herndon Barbershop on Peachtree to its employees, supporting the NAACP, and providing bail money anonymously for civil rights workers in Atlanta.

Ty Cobb, the Georgia Peach, was the first baseball player inducted into the Baseball Hall of Fame. He played for the Detroit Tigers, but came back to Georgia and lived in Atlanta after he retired.

Bobby Jones was the greatest golfer of his time, amateur or professional. He is the only golfer to win the Grand Slam in a single year, and was so widely idolized that he attracted thousands of people to take up the game of golf. He founded the Masters Tournament in Augusta, but lived in Atlanta.

Margaret Mitchell was a reporter for the Atlanta *Constitution* who, like many reporters, worked on a novel on the side. The novel, *Gone With the Wind,* quickly became a bestseller. The movie broke all box office records when it premiered in 1939—in Atlanta.

Martin Luther King, Jr. grew up in Atlanta, entered the ministry, and became the torchbearer for the civil rights movement throughout the country. It was his influence that kept the civil rights movement in this country primarily nonviolent. In 1962, he won the Nobel Peace Prize. In 1968 he was assassinated.

Living Legends

In a metropolitan area of 3 million people, it is hard to know who is a living legend and who is only a falling star. It is also sometimes hard to know who to count. Is **Julia Roberts** still a local girl, or is she now a Hollywood transplant? What about **Kim Basinger?** She owned the whole town of Braselton, but then lost that big lawsuit. Fortune can be as fleeting as fame.

At Kudzu Undercover, we believe that a living legend must be known by at least two generations and still be alive—or at least rumored as such—to qualify. Here is our list:

Jane wants you to work out...

James Earl Carter, better known as Jimmy, former governor of Georgia and President of the United States. It is hard to determine whether Carter lives in Atlanta or in Plains, but the location of his Presidential library in Virginia Highlands tips the scale in favor of Atlanta. He often pops up with hammer in hand to build low cost housing, and sometimes invites old—and new—buddies to town to help drive a few nails. He's our bet for lighting the torch at the Olympics, if anyone at ACOG has enough sway to talk him into it.

Another sentimental favorite for lighting the torch or doing something monumental during the Olympics would be **Coretta Scott King,** the widow of Martin Luther King, Jr. Mrs. King is the president of the King Center for Social Change and has gained great stature since the death of her husband.

It is to be hoped that **James Dickey** is already rehearsing rhymes for Zeus and discus in preparation for penning a tribute to the Olympics, as he did following the landing of the astronauts on the moon. Dickey is the South's strongest voice in literature at present and has an impressive body of poetry to his credit, as well as the novel *Deliverance.* Dickey was born in Atlanta.

One of the most well-known of all Atlantans is **Ted Turner,** who turned a billboard company into a broadcasting and sports empire. Turner is owner of the Atlanta Braves and Hawks, as well as Cable News Network, WTBS, Sports South, and TNT. He owns the MGM film library, the most extensive body of films extant. Lately, he has also pursued a body of films of a different kind, wooing and wedding **Jane Fonda,** who gained fame for her work in such Hollywood classics as *Barbarella* and *Moon Over Hanoi.* More recently, Jane has been the guru of fitness videos. Together, Ted and Jane are promoting buffalo meat as an alternative to beef. They own a buffalo herd.

Evander Holyfield continues to work toward regaining the world heavyweight boxing title that he won and lost within the space of a year.

Elton John scoots in and out of Atlanta, usually without any fanfare.

Don Sutton is now known more for his permanent wave and Carpets of Dalton than for his pitching heroics for the Dodgers, which got him elected to the Hall of Fame.

And a living legend among cats, although unknown to most humans, is **Waldo Japussy,** the author of the best-selling book *The Tao of Meow.* Waldo lives in Alpharetta and is chief feline on the Kudzu Undercover squad.

...Waldo prefers step aerobics

Anthony's Plantation

The illusion is almost perfect. As you sit at your table on the enclosed, second story porch at Anthony's Plantation, sipping on a wine just brought from their extensive cellar, looking out over the lush grounds, it is almost as if you had taken a time machine back to antebellum Georgia. This is your plantation. You have just ridden back from Savannah, where you had been engaged in commerce, and now you are home, celebrating your achievements.

Then your imagination flashes you a few years forward. You are off to war, to defend your plantation. While you are gone, Sherman's troops ride their horses through the main hallway of the mansion, but they do not burn or destroy it. The home is saved in deference to the pleas of your pregnant wife.

The reverie is shattered by the waiter bringing the first course. Madame is having a four-cheese pie, which sates her pizza lust; the gentleman is having a reggae shrimp salad. A huge mound of shrimp is blended with a coconut dressing and surrounded by fresh slices of mango, pineapple, and peach. It is wonderful.

Service is superb

In 1960, this venerable plantation home lay deserted in Washington, Georgia, two hours to the east. It was literally falling down, waiting for the kudzu to creep in and finish it off. But then it got a reprieve; it was dismantled board for board, brought to Buckhead, and reassembled exactly as it was in its prime—to serve as home for a new restaurant.

Since then, additional rooms have been added, but all the charm of the original has been left intact. Just strolling through the rooms and seeing the artifacts and art collected there is a treat in itself.

Madame ordered the Chateaubriand, which is served with a Marchand du Vin sauce and vegetables. Normally, it is sliced tableside from a marvelous rolling sideboard called "the Silver Chariot." The Chariot was resting that night, however, so we got the beef but not the show.

The gentleman ordered the Veal Anthony, which is a large veal chop stuffed with shrimp and crab. Both entrées were superb, as were the accompaniments: an excellent scallop of potato and mushrooms, plus gently sauteed sticks of carrot and asparagus.

Be sure to leave room for a dessert soufflé. Chocolate and vanilla are standard, but we opted for the evening's specialty—a berry soufflé that was berry, berry good.

The service is impeccable. The food is contemporary Southern and the ambience is from another world. Pricing is moderately expensive, but an excellent value for what they serve.

Anthony's can be found on lovely grounds in the heart of Buckhead at 3109 Piedmont Road. Call 262-7379 for reservations.

Diners enjoy the repast on the second story porch

Wild About Harry's

If you are new to Atlanta, or just visiting, this may be a concept that is hard to imagine:

A grocery store the size of a city block, filled with fresh produce, fish, meat, and baked goods from all over the world.

A grocery store where the broccoli is piled 10 feet high, and every head is in perfect condition.

A grocery store where you can buy fruits and vegetables one at a time—or by the case.

A grocery store where you can buy fresh, ripe corn on the cob year round. In off season, they fly it in from Mexico or Peru.

A grocery store where you can actually buy a rack of lamb—or have chops cut to your order.

A grocery store where you can choose from well over 100 square feet of shrimp.

A grocery store where you can buy freshly prepared sushi.

A grocery store where you can sip on a cappucino while you shop.

A grocery store where they bake all their breads fresh daily, and offer everything from an excellent French bread to foccaccia and Mongolian flat bread.

This is Harry's Market. The original is in Alpharetta; others are popping up all over the

The Roma tomatoes are ripe and succulent

north side. Harry also has some smaller, specialty shops in Buckhead and elsewhere called "Harry's in a Hurry."

Every big city should have a Harry's; the fact that Atlanta has several, plus the DeKalb Farmer's Market (where Harry first tested his concepts), and no other city has one, is remarkable.

The sheer range of food items available at Harry's is staggering. You can find Japanese eggplant just as easily as snap beans here; if you like green peas (English peas here), they have already shelled them for you. In recent months, we have found miniature asparagus from Chile and genuine French green beans—grown that way, not sliced to imitate them.

Quite understandably, the volume of business Harry does is immense. Customers flock in from all over the region. On any given day, it seems as though the entire foreign population of Atlanta is shopping at Harry's, because of the incredible variety of ethnic and specialty foods.

Best of all, the prices are likely to be the lowest you can find in Atlanta. Harry's does not advertise itself as a discount food store, but where he saves money, he does pass the savings along in terms of pricing.

One of the best features of Harry's is "Harry's in a Hurry." You can buy a whole quiche ready to cook—the gruyere cheese with dill quiche easily beats out most restaurant quiches. Or you can buy a meal that's been already cooked, such as lasagna or sliced roast pork with corn. Harry's has even provided freshly-baked desserts—whole tarts and cakes.

Harry's is open until 8 p.m. Monday through Friday, until 9 p.m. on Saturday, and until 7 p.m. on Sunday. The Alpharetta store is located on Upper Hembree Road, just a block south of its intersection with Route 9.

Whether a resident or a visitor, don't miss out on Harry's. It's a one of a kind experience.

The front entrance to Harry's

Pumpkins for sale, as well as plants of every kind

The Herndon Home

Sitting high on a hilltop on the west side of Downtown, with a magnificent view of Atlanta's skyline, the Alonzo Herndon home is one of this city's great treasures.

Alonzo Herndon was born a slave in Social Circle, Georgia. After being freed, he worked as a field laborer and then a barber. Saving his earnings, he moved to Atlanta as a young man and opened his own barber shop. His business sense let him expand to where he owned three shops, one of them the most elegant in the country.

Already a millionaire by the turn of the century, Herndon was approached in 1905 to help prevent various black insurance companies from failing. He invested in them, created the Atlanta Life Insurance Company, and guided it to becoming one of the most successful black-owned businesses in the country. Its impressive headquarters on Auburn Street testifies to its success.

Herndon and his wife Adrienne, director of the drama department at Atlanta University, designed the Herndon home themselves, choosing a Beaux Arts classical style. After two years of construction, it was finished in 1910. Tragically, Adrienne died just days after moving into the new home.

The beauty of this house lies not only in the design, but even more so in the details. The stair newells are wooden lion heads hand carved by Cliff Nelms. The wood floors form intricate designs with subtle shifts from room to room. An immense built-in sideboard in the dining room is a gorgeous piece of craftsmanship.

The chandelier in the middle of the main stairwell consists of little cherubs carrying torches. Did Herndon anticipate the Olympics 90 years ago?

After Adrienne died, Herndon married again. Alonzo died in 1927; Jessica in 1947. Norris, the only child of Alonzo and Adrienne, continued to live in the house until his death in 1977.

At that time the house was deeded over to the Herndon Foundation, to preserve it as an icon of black achievement.

Tours of this remarkable house are free and require no advance reservation, except for groups. The house is on display 10 a.m. to 4 p.m. Tuesdays through Saturdays.

It is located at 587 University Place. Drive west from Downtown on Martin Luther King Drive. Turn right on Vine St. at the top of the hill, then right again on University.

A copy of *Time* bearing Martin Luther King, Jr.'s signature

Free At Last

The career of Martin Luther King, Jr., is larger than life; it has assumed almost legendary proportions. The boy who grew up on Auburn Avenue in Atlanta, followed his father's and his grandfather's footsteps in both entering the ministry and fighting for civil rights, has become a symbol for blacks throughout the world: a symbol of courage and dedication. Just so, the area on Auburn Street that begins with the Ebenezer Baptist Church, where three generations of Kings preached, and ends with his birthplace home, has become a shrine which has attracted pilgrims from all over the globe.

The heart of the shrine is the King Center for Social Change, which also houses the King Memorial. Dr. King's body lies in a stately tomb in the middle of a long pool of cascading waters. At one end is a small, nondenominational chapel; the rest of the memorial is surrounded by the Center for Social Change and Freedom Hall, a community gathering place.

Birthhome of Martin Luther King, Jr.

The King Memorial

Inside the center, there is a retrospective on King's life, and a few exhibits—ministerial robes, traveling clothes, and so on. These areas are maintained by the National Park Service, which also offers tours of King's birthplace. The offices of the center are not open to the public.

In Freedom Hall, there is a small room in memory of Mahatma Gandhi, the Indian guru who inspired King's strict adherence to nonviolent means for social change.

A bust of Gandhi

It is easy to forget how much King accomplished before he was slain. Having been honored with the Nobel Peace Prize, he was named by *Time* as Man of the Year. These achievements signaled an acceptance of the civil rights movement which opened the doors for rapid social change, not only here in Atlanta but throughout the nation—and the world. It was only after King won the Peace Prize, for instance, that black and white community leaders in Atlanta finally sat down at a formal dinner together—to honor King.

The King Memorial has meaning for both blacks and whites. For blacks, it is a shrine that unifies them and inspires them. For whites, it is an opportunity to learn more about King and the struggles he faced.

The King Memorial is at 449 Auburn Avenue.

A Playground of Science

The word "science" means knowledge. SciTrek, then, is a trip into the roots of what is known—specifically, the known principles of physical life. It also happens to be a wonderful way for children to get first-hand experience with the scientific principles governing life.

Technically, SciTrek is a museum, but that is not really the best description. It is actually more of a scientific playground, where kids can learn that science is fun. In various interactive displays, kids learn that:

- Science can make your hair stand on end.
- Science can help your friends appear to levitate.
- Science can let you lift an automobile engine with one hand.
- Science can enable you to generate electricity just by riding a bicycle.

These are all interactive displays designed to lure school children into a greater fascination with the beauty and genius of science. In addition, one whole area of the museum is reserved for younger children, where they can literally play at science.

Here they can pretend to be a TV weatherperson giving a broadcast—and see themselves on a monitor as they give their performance! They can learn to do electronic finger painting on a computer—or make waves in a big wave machine.

Each toy is designed to teach children a basic scientific principle—by doing, rather than memorizing.

SciTrek also features regular traveling exhibits.

The museum is located in the Atlanta Civic Center at 395 Piedmont Ave. (Piedmont and Pine). It is open Tuesdays through Saturdays 10 to 5 and Sunday 12 to 5.

The Eiffel Tower recreated by Erector set

This girl can talk to a friend 100 feet away just by whispering. The parabola throws her voice to another one across the room.

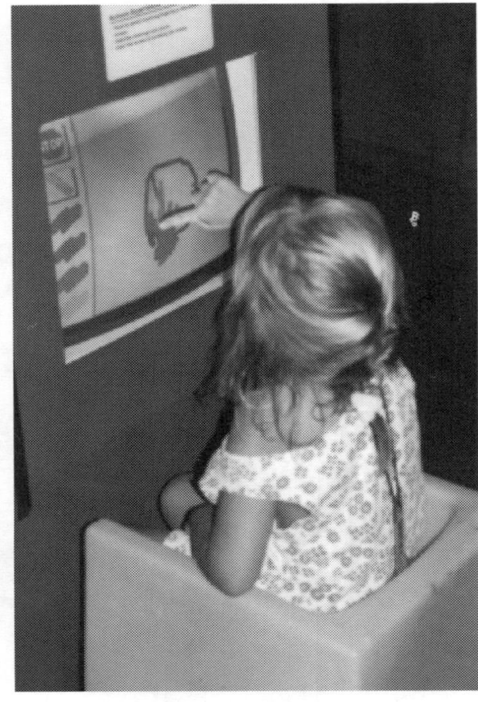
Electronic finger painting

Boot, Scoot & Boogie

The band rips into a Texas Two Step; Miss Rebecca demonstrates the Boot, Scoot, & Boogie

It does not take long to discover that the music of popular choice in Atlanta is Country & Western. Nashville may be the home of the Grand Ole Opry, but Atlanta has certainly given her heart to this kind of music as well.

For proof, just visit Miss Kitty's Dance Hall and Saloon any night of the week. But don't show up in shorts, looking like a dude. Dress like a cowboy or cowgirl. Jeans will do, but boots and the right kind of hat give you far more credibility.

At 8, there is hardly anyone in the place. By 9, when the band shows up and starts playing, the place is packed. There are some beginners, but most of the dancers are quite accomplished. They whirl and twirl their way around the dance floor, as the band plays the hits of the day, plus their own compositions.

This is high energy music and high energy dancing. The band raises the rafters every night of the week.

Beer is the beverage of choice here.

If you are unfamiliar with country dancing, you may wish to show up at 8 on a Monday or Tuesday night, when Miss Rebecca gives free lessons in the Texas Two-Step and the Boot, Scoot, and Boogie.

Couples take a turn on the floor; beginners learn the Two Step

The ladies do seem to outnumber the gents, which ought to make this an ideal place for a lonely guy to dance his way into some girl's heart. For guys who get too tired to dance, Miss Kitty has thoughtfully provided a number of pool tables upstairs.

Miss Kitty's is located at 1038 Franklin Rd. in Marietta. Take I-75 north of the Perimeter to Delk Road, turn left on Delk, and then right on Franklin. The phone is 426-9077.

Surin of Thailand

For folks who are as yet unfamiliar with Thai cuisine, it is very much like Chinese, but often more subtle and delicate. Due to the strong Asian community in Atlanta, there is an abundance of very good Thai restaurants to choose from. If you are looking for the best, however, the consensus vote strongly favors Surin of Thailand.

Surin is the name of the chef, and his modest restaurant is located at the corner of Highland Avenue and Greenwood Avenue in the heart of the Virginia Highlands neighborhood.

Do not let first impressions fool you. The deep blue tablecloths are a welcomed relief from the typical Chinese red, but the tables are lined up as though he were serving an officers' mess—folks in quest of a memorable dining experience. Nevertheless, the palate quickly overrules the eyes. One bite of anything on the menu and you will realize that Surin's talent and creativity lie solidly in the kitchen.

For an appetizer, try either one of Surin's outstanding soups, which are served over a volcano burner and are more than enough for two, or the ka proud rolls, which are seafood and Thai basil all wrapped up and shaped like egg rolls, although they are not deep fried.

From the first bite on, your mouth will know that you are eating one of the most sublime creations ever produced in a kitchen. But be warned—these rolls are decidedly spicy. You might not think so on the first or second bite, but before you have polished off the second roll, you will be reaching for all the water or beer you can find.

A banner of Buddha adorns Surin of Thailand

The bar at Surin's

Incidentally, the Thai beer Sing Ha (pronounced Sing High) is an excellent accompaniment to the spicy Thai cuisine. It has a cooling edge to it that is lacking in domestic beers.

For dinner, our party had spicy spaghetti, ka proud lamb, and spicy basil chicken. The spicy spaghetti is a Chef Surin original. It is a bowl of homemade, thick spaghetti noodles tossed with shrimp, chicken, tomatoes, mushrooms, and an array of Thai spices. If you are expecting industrial strength tomato sauce and a meatball, this is not for you. But if you want something a bit exotic, this is a good choice. It is definitely hot.

The ka proud lamb is half of a rack of lamb, split and grilled, basted with ka proud sauce. It was superb and only mildly hot. The spicy basil chicken was the closest to a Chinese-style dish—thin strips of chicken (beef or shrimp are also available) are sautéed in a spicy sauce with lots of julienned vegetables. It was very tasty.

Only two desserts are offered, but these folks know what they are doing. Both the coconut and the mango ice creams are excellent—and both are exactly what your mouth needs so that you will not incinerate your loved one or date when you kiss him or her later in the evening. Be sure to complete the meal with one or the other of these heavenly ice creams.

Hammerin' Hank

Quickly now. Which two major league baseball players hit their 714th home runs while wearing a Braves uniform? The answer: both Babe Ruth and Henry Aaron. Aaron, of course, went on to hit number 715—plus 40 more.

Aaron accomplished his heroic feat as an Atlanta Brave. Ruth did it as a Boston Brave—even though he hit the vast majority of his homers as a New York Yankee. Ruth's record stood for more than 30 years. Aaron's monumental total of 755 may well stand for a good while longer. In fact, it has already been almost 20 years.

Henry Aaron played for the Braves, first in Milwaukee and then in Atlanta, during an era that was dominated by Mickey Mantle and Willie Mays. They got more headlines than Aaron did, but in the end, Hammerin' Hank got more home runs—and the biggest headlines of all.

Aaron is still associated with the Braves, serving as vice-president for the club. But he keeps a low profile now; his bat is silent.

Aaron had a natural feel for every phase of the game. He has said that when he was hitting, he would instinctively know what kind of pitch the pitcher was going to throw at him, even before he released it.

It takes this level of inspiration and ability to be able to set a record such as 755 home runs.

In a few years, the Braves will not even be playing in the stadium where Henry Aaron smacked No. 715. But the impact will still be felt for many, many years.

THE ATLANTA CONSTITUTION

For 105 Years the South's Standard Newspaper

VOL. 106, No. 230 P. O. Box 4689 ATLANTA, GA. 30302, TUESDAY, APRIL 9, 1974 68 PAGES, 3 SECTIONS TEN CENTS

Aaron Hammers No. 715 And Moves Ahead of Ruth

NEWS THIS MORNING

WORLD

NATION

By WAYNE MINSHEW

The Appalachian Trail

One of the most unusual feats (pardon the pun) constructed by mankind is the 2,150-mile Appalachian Trail, which lets the industrious hiker walk all the way from northern Georgia to the middle of Maine, following the crest of the Appalachian Mountains—or any shorter segment of the same.

The true beginning of the trail is on the top of Springer Mountain, a few miles north of Dawsonville. But for all practical purposes the beginning is the ranger station at Amicalola Falls State Park, nine miles away. For if you plan to hike the trail, it is important to sign in with the park ranger. Also, the eight-mile trail to the top of Springer Mountain is the only trail leading to it.

Southern starting point of Appalachian Trail

This is no overnight hike. If you were able to average 20 miles a day—and remember, the trail goes up and down the crest of the mountains—it would take 108 days to make the complete trip. There are primitive shelters scattered every seven or eight miles along the trail, but there are also apt to be many nights spent without any kind of roof over your head. Occasionally, the trail takes you right down the middle of a sleepy town, as it does in Hanover, New Hampshire, but that is a rare occurrence. It does not intersect with any towns in Georgia, although it does pass within a mile or so of Suches, on State Route 60.

The top of Amicalola Falls

If you are one of those folks who would like to walk a few hundred yards along the trail, so that you can tell disbelieving relatives that you have actually hiked the Appalachian Trail, take U.S. 19 out of Dahlonega, then follow U.S. Route 129 another 9 or 10 miles to where the trail crosses the road.

For the more adventurous, spend a weekend at Amicalola Falls State Park. It has a brand new lodge, 14 rental cottages, and tent and trailer sites. If you love to hike, you can make a day's trek out of a round trip journey to Springer Mountain and back. If you prefer something less rigorous, take the 3 1/2 mile trail up to the falls and back to the ranger station.

Amicalola means "tumbling waters" in Cherokee, and the 729-foot falls do just that. The tallest falls in the state, they are a gorgeous site to behold.

To get to the park, take Route 52 west of Dahlonega.

The state has a very complete network of parks throughout Georgia, making it easy for Georgians to take advantage of the natural beauty and resources to be found from the mountains to the coastline.

Tanner's

When Atlanta *Constitution* Editor Henry Grady coined the phrase "The New South" more than 100 years ago, he was probably not referring to a type of cooking. But if the label fits, why not swear by it?

It certainly fits at Tanner's, an Atlanta-based chain of restaurants specializing in chicken rotisserie. The old Southern tradition, fried chicken, has been replaced by a new Southern tradition, chicken that has been roasted slowly on a turning spit. You can order either a 1/4 or 1/2 of the bird, depending on the size of your stomach.

Few foods can compare with the taste of roasted chicken, unless you adorn them with sauces or seasonings. Rotisserie chicken is delicious served right from the spit.

For those who cannot divorce themselves fully from fried chicken, Tanner's does offer "chicken fingers," which are strips of chicken breasts that are breaded and deep fried. They are served with a honey mustard sauce for dipping. They are like manna from heaven.

One more chicken dish deserves mention: Tanner's rotisserie chicken sandwich, which is quite possibly the best hot chicken sandwich available. You can also get orders of chicken lips and bubba wings as appetizers, if you desire.

The one food item conspicuously absent from the menu is beef. This is not an accidental oversight; the menu clearly refers to a chicken sandwich as the "Unbeef Sandwich."

This is not to imply that Tanner's is a one-bird eatery. They have recently added a turkey platter which may just be the best development of the year—a huge portion of sliced turkey breast resting on a mound of cornbread stuffing and served with a choice of two vegetables. The fried jumbo shrimp are easily the best fried shrimp in town, and what can one say about the ribs? They are outstanding.

Chicken on the spit

For folks who cannot make up their minds, Tanner's lets you make up a combination plate with two or three different meat items, plus sides.

And don't take the sides lightly, either. True to its Southern heritage, Tanner's offers a wide variety of veggies every day—blackeyed peas, a zucchini squash soufflé, creamed spinach, corn, and—yes, turnip greens.

Service is friendly and the prices are inexpensive. It is popular with families and casual diners—and just about everyone else who likes good food.

Tanner's would get a big thumbs up—except that chickens don't have thumbs any more than they have lips.

Tanner's can be found at numerous locations in the metro area.

Hot Shots

On target at P.O.'d Palomas

Steve Middleditch conducts a lesson

Every weekend morning, millions of guys tell their spouses, "Honey, I'm going out to shoot a round of golf." If the folks at Cherokee Rose have their way, that line will gradually be changing to: "Honey, I'm going out to shoot a few dozen clays."

Cherokee Rose is a shooting resort—probably the finest in the world, according to many experts. Located in Griffin, just 30 minutes south of Hartsfield, it is dedicated to popularizing the growing sport of "sporting clays."

Sporting clays takes the old idea of skeet shooting and turns it into a sport. It resembles skeet in that clay rounds are launched into the air as targets to be shot down. But it differs from skeet shooting as much as an hour's practice on the driving range differs from playing 18 holes of golf.

A game of sporting clays involves walking through the woods from station to station. At each station, clay targets are launched into the air from a variety of angles, each to be shot at by the marksmen. Points are scored for direct hits—when the target explodes in a puff of smoke.

Once each shooter has had a chance with all of the options at a station, the party moves on to the next station and tries its luck there. Each station is designed to simulate the challenges of one particular kind of hunting. At "Humpin' Hares," for example, the clay targets are launched from the side of the target area and actually bounce very rapidly across the ground, simulating the hopping movement of rabbits. At the duck pond area, the shooters must take aim from behind a blind, as you would in actual duck hunting.

The main entrance

One of the stations

But all of the shooting at Cherokee Rose is done with clay targets. No animals are involved. In fact, Cherokee Rose is designated as a wildlife sanctuary. In spite of the gun fire, the deer, squirrels, and birds that live here seem to know they are protected.

In all, the sporting clay course at Cherokee Rose consists of 10 stations and requires about 2 hours to complete. Each station has been given a clever name based on the type of hunting it imitates: Turbo Woodchuck, Grouse Gulch, or Redneck Ringnecks.

The resort is not limited to just one bird in the bush, however. It provides a variety of other shooting sports, from Five Stand Sporting and Gattlinguns to Starshot, a huge target that rises out of the ground and resembles a fireworks display. It's a game that is best played at night. Cherokee Rose is one of four resorts in the country that has it.

You can even shoot skeet, if you want to, or practice marksmanship on a rifle and pistol range.

In addition to the games, Cherokee Rose offers instruction by appointment. The shooting school is run by Steve Middleditch, a transplant from Dorset County, England, and the 1990 World Professional Clay Target Champion.

As in golf, as much money can be spent on guns and shot in this sport as on the fees to use the course. There is a well stocked pro shop to serve the needs of the shooters using the facilities. There is also a restaurant on premises that serves lunch every day and dinner on Friday and Saturday nights. The food is excellent. In fact, if you like quail, you might want to drive out to Cherokee Rose just to eat at the Winchester Café.

The grounds are saturated with the rich natural beauty of the Georgia woodlands. The course takes advantage of the natural contours of the land, instead of being imposed upon it. The result is a shooting course that is fun, challenging, and picturesque. It's enough to make a person pick up a gun and try shooting.

Cherokee Rose is open to the public. Fees to use the course are roughly comparable to a round of golf at one of the better golf courses around Atlanta. Memberships are available for frequent users.

The resort is also willing to customize shooting packages for corporations and groups that wish to schedule an outing. The number to call is 228-2529.

To reach Cherokee Rose, take I-75 South to Highway 19; follow it south for 14 miles to Birdie Road, the third blinking yellow light after the Atlanta Motor Speedway. Turn left and go 2 miles on Birdie Road. Cherokee Rose will be on the left.

Taking aim at "Ass O' Woodies"

Winchester Café serves excellent food

The pro shop can meet any shooting need

Golfing Atlanta

Teeing off at Cross Creek; gazing down the fairway from the 17th tee at Country Land

Golf, at its highest level, is meant to be a pleasing afternoon adventure that tests the golfer's skill while refreshing his or her body and soul. The metro Atlanta area is blessed to have an abundance of courses which blend beauty and challenge.

Traditionally, many of the finest courses in and around Atlanta have been private clubs, which could only be played by members and guests. The private clubs still dominate, to be sure, but every year brings a greater variety of public courses as well—many of them first-rate.

The history of golf in Atlanta is a fabled one, dominated by the legendary Bobby Jones, who made his home here. One of the few public courses within the city of Atlanta is, indeed, the Bobby Jones Golf Course at 384 Woodward Way, just off Northside Drive in the near northwest part of the city. It was founded by Jones himself; Peachtree Creek meanders through the course. At 6150 yards in length, it plays to a par 71. Greens fees are very reasonable.

For beginners and golfers who wish to work on their short game, the course to check out is the Cross Creek Country Club, which is just a short distance from the Moores Mill exit on I-75 north. This is a challenging par 3, 18-hole course that can be played walking (they have no carts for rent) in a couple of hours. No hole is longer than 140 yards, making it a great course for people still learning to play—and inexpensive as well.

At the other end of the spectrum are daily fees courses that seek to compete with the established private clubs, offering such country club touches as bag drop off and pick up. Eagle Watch, just west of I-575 in Woodstock, is an outstanding example of this new breed of golf course. Designed just four years ago by the great Arnold Palmer, the greens and fairways are immaculately manicured. If you can keep the ball in the fairway on this course, you should be able to play at the top of your game. But this kind of golfing ex-

A fairway on one of three courses at Callaway Gardens

Approaching the 4th green at Marietta Club, with Kennesaw Mountain in the background

perience does not come cheaply. With the cost of the required cart included, the price of a round for two people tops $100.

One of the most exciting developments on the local golf scene has been the steady increase of resort golf courses in the area. The biggest complex is at Callaway Gardens, where a total of three 18-hole courses are available for use by people staying at the resort—and the public as well.

Closer by, several resorts at Lake Lanier offer excellent golf layouts for the use of their visitors, as well as the general public. Further north, resorts at Helen and Lake Arrowhead have courses that can be played by the public on a daily fees basis, as well as people staying at the resort. Several more projects in the Atlanta area which will include resort golf layouts have recently been announced as well.

In addition to these courses, there are lots of other clubs and courses to choose from, in every part of metro Atlanta—and the surrounding areas. Some, like the City Club of Marietta, are run by the cities where they are located. The Marietta course is a hilly one with tight fairways and a fair amount of water. It is a good example of what a typical course in north Georgia should be like—lots of ups and downs. It costs about $60 for two people to play with a rented cart.

To the north, about an hour from downtown Atlanta, Country Land is an outstanding public golf course—and already ranked among the top 50 public courses in Georgia, even though it is only a few years old. It plays at par 70 for 6000 yards and includes some of the most daunting uphill shots you can find anywhere.

Generally speaking, golf courses on the north side of Atlanta will be hilly and tight. On the south side, they will tend to be more level and open. As a result, the courses on the southern side will tend to employ more sand traps to challenge the golfer, while courses on the northern side usually have plenty of built-in, natural challenges.

Due to the semi-tropical weather, golf courses in the Altanta area are open for play year around. In fact, all but the hardiest golfers tend to stay at home in midsummer, when the temperature soars above 90°. Far more will flock out for a round on mild days in December or January—and there are plenty of them.

The ability to play golf year round has helped places such as the Peachtree Executive Conference Center, which operates the Brae Linn course in Peachtree City, a private club that is also open for resort play for visitors at the center. Winter golf is a big plus in drawing business meetings and conferences to the Atlanta area.

With more than 60 courses to choose from in the metro area, it is no longer necessary to plan a golf retreat to the shore. Great golfing variety is right at hand, within an hour's drive.

Bunkers guard the greens at Eagles Watch

Lickskillet Farm

Atlanta is filled with charming spots, little oases of Mother Nature nestled in an untouched nook or cranny of the metropolitan area. It's a delight to visit these places and just stand there in silence. The illusion of being in the midst of the wilderness is almost complete, except that you could walk a half mile in any direction and stumble back into the "real world" of the city.

One of the most delightful of these havens from concrete and noise is the Lickskillet Farm, a quiet, secluded restaurant in the grand tradition of Southern hospitality just two minutes from Georgia 400 in Roswell.

What a difference two minutes can make! One moment you are traveling north on 400, sharing scowls and stares with thousands of other weary commuters on their way home; the next, you are wandering through the gardens at Lickskillet, a glass of Chardonnay in hand, letting the cares of the day roll away as you watch the ripples of water flow down Foe Killer Creek.

Foe Killer Creek was originally Four Killer Creek, named for the Cherokee Indian who originally owned the land at the creek's headwaters. After a generation or two of the Southern drawl, it became Foe Killer. One can presume that the four men Four Killer killed were foes.

The restaurant, of course, is indoors, in a home built in the early 1800's. But the hosts encourage guests who want to stretch their legs before dining to amble about the spacious grounds. Sit a while and sip your wine. Look for the remains of the old mill. When you are ready to enjoy the meal, come on back up to the house.

Lickskillet, viewed from the creek

Dining in the patio room

And you will enjoy the meal. The menu is enough to make anyone's mouth water, and the food is expertly prepared. In many cases, the herbs and vegetables come right out of the kitchen garden behind the house.

We ordered a wheel of cracklin' cornbread, which we munched on contentedly as the soups and salads were brought. The lobster bisque was quite good, and the two salads were fresh and zesty.

For our entrées, we ordered the Cornish hen and the filet mignon. The Cornish hen turned out to be one of those special dishes that make you want to keep on coming back to a restaurant over and over again. It had been butterflied and marinated in rosemary, sage, and red wine, then grilled and served with a plum sauce. The filet was an excellent piece of beef, charbroiled and served with a good bearnaise sauce.

Service was very good, and the ambience of the old country home enriches the dining experience. We ate in a porch room that has been added on, overlooking the gardens and creek, but the main room is even more cozy and quaint.

Lickskillet Farms is at 1380 Old Roswell Road. Call at 475-6484.

Knightmare at the Omni

One of the brightest shining new stars on the Atlanta sports scene is the Atlanta Knights, an expansion team in the International Hockey League last year. In spite of it being their maiden year, the Knights ended up with an impressive winning season of 53-23-7, second best in the IHL, and won the Atlantic Division title. They also made it to the second round of the league's playoffs, where they lost to the eventual winner, the Ft. Wayne Komets.

As a minor league team, the Knights are affiliated with the Tampa Bay Lightning, which was itself an expansion team in the National Hockey League. As a result, the playing personnel of the team will vary a great deal from season to season, as more talented and experienced players are promoted to the big time.

One of the most talked about players on the squad last year was Manon Rheaume, who made professional sport history in 1992 when she became the first woman ever to play a game at the major league level of any sport. She started in goal for Tampa in a game against the St. Louis Blues, making seven saves on nine shots against goal in the 20-minute period she played.

For the Knights, she appeared in two regular season games, making three saves out of fours shots in the first and 27 saves out of 33 shots in the second.

With the Knights getting off to such an impressive start, the future of ice hockey in Atlanta looks brighter than 15 years ago, when the Atlanta Flames were the local entry into the NHL—only to move on to Calgary, Canada, where ice is easier to come by.

Indeed, attendance at the Knights' games increased steadily throughout the year, as the team established themselves as a contender. Between November and March, average attendance at a Knight's game doubled.

In many ways, hockey is the most graceful and exhilarating of all major sports. The action unfolds quickly as two or three skaters rush down the ice, flipping the puck back and forth, until one of them takes a shot on goal. If the propensity of hockey players to mix things up in brawls and full body slams could be curtailed, hockey's popularity could easily improve tremendously.

The Knights seem eager to encourage such popular support for hockey in Atlanta. During the summer off-season, they have joined with the Boy and Girls Clubs of Atlanta to sponsor "street hockey." In lieu of ice—a rare commodity in metro Atlanta—the game is played on the street—or in a gym.

The program is designed not only to "keep Atlanta's kids off the streets by putting them on the street," but also to heighten local awareness of the Knights and the game of hockey.

For information about the Knight's schedule and tickets, call 525-8900.

Photos courtesy the Atlanta Knights

Fernbank

A dinosaur mother and her eggs

From the moment you first set foot into the new Fernbank Museum of Natural History, you know you are entering someplace special. Even though it is a science museum, it is almost as though you are actually setting foot in God's private gallery, where He comes to look at Creation and marvel at what He has done.

The building is certainly majestic enough. Outside, it looks as though you are approaching a Renaissance Italian palace. Inside, a colonnaded foyer leads to a stunning, three-story circular atrium or Great Hall, around which the museum unfolds. The atrium is large enough to seat hundreds of people for special events, although it is usually empty.

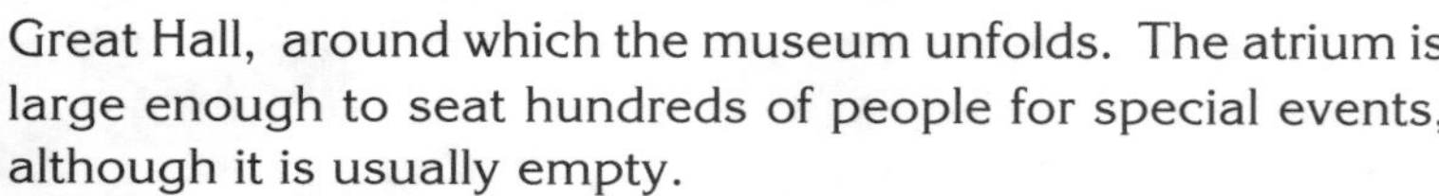

The building was built with great care. The tile on which you walk is as much a part of the museum's display as anything behind glass. It is cut from marble that contains fossils of

A schoolgirl and a big bubble

Exploring the musical scale

ancient life forms. As you walk through the museum, therefore, you are literally walking back through time, toward the beginning of Creation.

The exhibits at Fernbank are every bit as impressive. There is none of the stuffy atmosphere that you find in many of the older museums of natural history around the country; the Fernbank is a thoroughly modern museum. And fun.

The Tornado

In one gallery, for example, is the Spectrum of the Senses, which demonstrates the physical laws of sight and sound in a most spectacular way. In one exhibit, a tornado is created every 30 seconds or so; in another, a black and white disk creates the spectrum of color as it whirls at various speeds.

In another hall, A Walk through Time in Georgia recreates the evolution of natural history in Georgia—from seacoast to mountains—since the beginning of time. It includes an impressive dinosaur exhibit and a recreation of the Okefenokee Swamp which is breathtaking—and spooky.

Another outstanding permanent feature at the museum is The World of Shells, the superb collection of Richard S. and Lella Maurer. The collection contains some of the most beautiful and rare seashells in the world—an unusual visual delight. In addition, there is a thousand-gallon aquarium which contains a living coral reef demonstrating the vital role of mollusks in the oceanic world.

Fernbank also features an IMAX theater, a six-story theater which is the largest film format in the world. Films such as “Mountain Gorilla” and “Grand Canyon” play in the IMAX on a regular basis. There is also a large hall for traveling exhibits; during the summer of 1993, it contained the remarkable robotic dinosaur display, which was realistic enough to frighten any number of kids while we were there. These displays change periodically.

Two of the most creative portions of the museum are the Fantasy Forest, for small children, and Georgia Adventure, for kids 6-10. In Fantasy Forest, for example, children can learn how bees pollinate flowers and basic concepts about light and shadow. It is an impressive exhibit that encourages parents to get involved with their children as they interact with their imaginations.

The Fernbank Museum of Natural History is located in Druid Hills at 767 Clifton Road, just off Ponce de Leon Avenue. It is the latest outgrowth of Fernbank Forest, 65 acres of gardens and woods. For more about Fernbank, turn the page.

In Fantasy Forest

One Fantastic Classroom

Fernbank Forest is in existence today because its original owner recognized the value of this unique parcel of land and wanted to share it with Atlantans, especially for educational purposes. For years, the forest was simply left open to the public. But the demands of preserving the land in its natural integrity became too much. So a deal was cut. The trust which owned the land deeded five acres of it to the Dekalb school system so it could build a science center—and the science center would take over upkeep and preservation of the forest, on the proviso that the forest would remain open to the public.

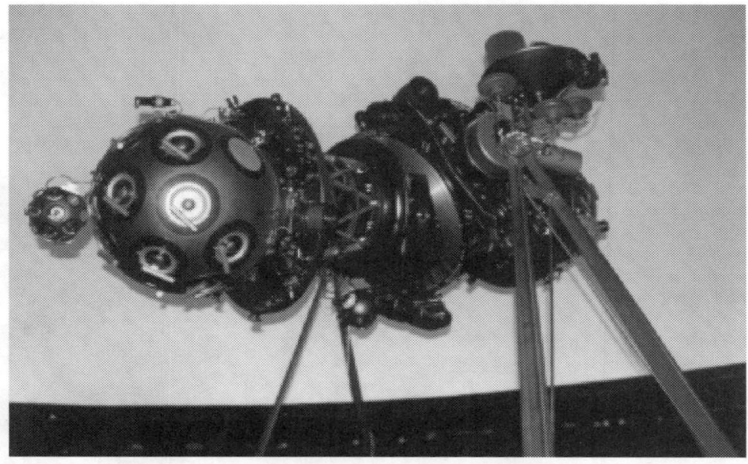

Not an alien spaceship—just the Planetarium's projector

The result is one of the most fantastic classrooms imaginable—a fully-equipped science center plus a 65-acre forest.

The forest is a magical place. Ample trails let you explore the forest leisurely and comfortably; visitors are asked to stay on the trails, to reduce the risk of possible damage. Unusual specimens are marked with signs along the edge of the trail.

One spot of special interest is a pond that forms itself out of one of the creeks running through the forest. It is a quiet place that draws you into its own peaceful communion and asks you why you haven't come to find rest here before—or why you do not come more often.

The forest is open Saturdays from 10 to 5, and from 2 to 5 on every other day. There is no charge to walk through the forest.

In the Science Center, the emphasis is far more on the skies than the forest. The Observatory boasts the largest telescope in the Southeast; it is open Thursday and Friday nights from darkness until 10:30, if the skies are clear.

Even more impressive, perhaps, is the Planetarium, with a 70-foot diameter dome and a collection of audio-visual equipment that defies imagination. This equipment is used to recreate the night sky for all to see—and study. Shows are held on a regular basis.

Fernbank Science Center is located at 156 Heaton Park Drive in Decatur. Call 378-4311.

A quiet pond in the Fernbank Forest; the Apollo 6 spacecraft on display at the science center

Fruit of the Vine

The grape is the heart of any vineyard. To the left, white varietal is ready for harvesting; above,a cluster of rich red grapes frames the Cavender Castle.

High atop Gold Hill, a couple of miles outside of Dahlonega in the north Georgia mountains, is an unusual way to get away from it all—the Cavender Castle Winery and Bed and Breakfast.

Georgia has never been known for its wines, but a growing number of dedicated wine growers throughout the state are trying to change that reputation. The problem with small wine growers is that most big wine distributors cannot be bothered with small lots. They want volume, no matter what the cost in taste. So the small wine grower must be ingenious in devising ways to market his or her product.

Wesley and Linda Phillips reason that if you cannot bring Mohammed to the mountain, then bring the mountain to Mohammed. In this case, they are bringing people to their winery through their bed and breakfast, one of the finest in the state.

For rates less than what you would expect to pay for a hotel room in downtown Atlanta, a couple or single guest can choose from among four guest rooms, each with a private bath. Since the castle is only a few years old, the rooms are all completely modern and elegantly decorated.

This is a great way to spend a romantic weekend—to celebrate an anniversary or spend a honeymoon. If you request it, a bottle of champagne and two glasses can be waiting for you in your guest room when you arrive. Then, in the morning, a complimentary breakfast by candelight continues the mood.

For some, the opportunity to relax with gorgeous views of the surrounding mountains may be all that they desire. For others, the sightseeing riches of Dahlonega offer plenty of daytime ad-

Wesley Phillips pours a sample of his wines

The private garden is an ideal place to relax; the living room gives you a chance to socialize

ventures. The Crisson Gold Mine is across the highway at the foot of the hill, a great place to learn to pan for gold. (And yes, there still is gold in the hills of Dahlonega.) Or you can drive into Dahlonega for shopping and sightseeing.

Sometime during the stay, however, you should check out the Cavender wines in their wine tasting room. Although the winery is too new to have produced wines from their own grapes—that will come as the years pass—they have nonetheless produced some very good wines using grapes bought from other vineyards. They have already won several prizes for their wines in competitions. Kudzu Undercover investigated their wines in some depth, and concurs.

And, if you are so inclined, the Phillips will be happy to sell you as much of their wine as you care to purchase, at very reasonable rates.

The Phillips also have a small gift shop connected with the wine tasting room, where they sell wine accessories, crafts, and other gifts. Even if you are not staying at the bed and breakfast, it is rewarding to stop just to taste—and buy—the wines.

Cavender Castle is located on Wimpy Mill Road, better known as U.S. 19 and Georgia 60 Connector. Take the entrance directly across from Crisson's, turn left, and follow the road to the top of Gold Hill. Call 1-706-864-4759 to make reservations for the bed and breakfast.

Cavender Castle is also available for catered parties and receptions.

Other wineries in the metro Atlanta area include Habersham's, in Baldwin; Chateau Elan, in Braselton; Chestnut Mountain, in Braselton; and Fox Vineyards, in Social Circle. All offer wine tastings and are happy to sell their product.

Special touches make staying at the castle a delight; wines for sale at reasonable prices

Ray's on the River

It's late in the day. You are tired and worn out. You have made plans to have dinner at Ray's on the River. You arrive with your wife, only to find that there will be a half hour wait. Is this just another hassle?

No way—not at Ray's on the River. Get a drink and stroll down to the river—the Chattahoochee—and soak in the warmth of the setting sun dancing across the ripples in the water. Sit on one of the benches in the beautifully landscaped grounds and breathe away all the frustrations and cares of the day.

Let the river talk to you. When it is finished, it will tell you to go back inside. There, you can listen to live soft jazz in the bar until your table is ready—or after dinner, if you prefer. The jazz continues to 1 a.m.

Once you are seated, you should be able to see the sun disappear in the west and night fall on the river. Take your time—order an appetizer. The fried artichoke hearts are exceptionally good.

Ray's is primarily a seafood emporium, and as such features several fresh fish selections each day, in addition to their regular menu. The fish, we are happy to report, does not come out of the Chattahoochee, but is flown in daily—except for the Georgia trout, which we presume is trucked in.

Everything we tried was pleasing and delicious. Among the four of us dining, we tried the blackened fish Alexander, the shrimp fettucini, the stuffed flounder Mornay, and grilled salmon.

The blackened fish Alexander was a combination of shrimp and scallops served in a lobster sauce. The shrimp fettucini was served with a classic Alfredo sauce. The flounder was stuffed with a spicy crabmeat mixture, then topped with Mornay sauce. The salmon was grilled to perfection.

Each entrée was served with either a rice medley—which was outstanding—or a baked potato. Excellent sweet biscuits were also served.

Maine lobster is available at market price, as is a number of steaks and prime rib. Ray's encourages making up combinations between beef and any of the fish selections.

For reservations, call 955-1187. Ray's is located at 6700 Powers Ferry Rd., just west of the Powers Ferry exit on I-285.

A Great Spot To Gather

For the last year or so, the city of Atlanta has been trying to find a slogan that could carry it forward into the next century, an elegant turn of the phrase such as Henry Grady's from 100 years ago: "A brave and beautiful city." But alas, even though local pundits have labored long and hard, burning the midnight oil, they have been unable to hit upon a slogan that was met with universal acclaim.

Or even mild enthusiasm.

At Kudzu, we believe the reason why a new slogan has been giving official Atlanta so much grief is that they have been trying too hard. All that is necessary is to survey the city and its assets.

The airport.

An amazing number of hotels.

All sizes and shapes of convention facilities, auditoriums, stadiums, and public places.

Wonderful restaurants.

In fact, all of the many assets that made Atlanta such an obvious pick for the Olympics. Put them all together and what have you got?

A great convention city—a town where people from across the nation and the world can come together, meet, and then go home.

Atlanta — where the world comes together.

Whether or not it ever makes it as a slogan, it is certainly true—and it has been ever since the first Cotton States Exposition in 1881, which was a version of a World's Fair, but dedicated to the proposition of promoting the use of cotton throughout the world.

Atlanta has never quit promoting itself—and inviting others to come to Atlanta for its conferences and conventions.

This is big business, of course—quite probably the biggest industry in Atlanta. If you add up all the money spent each year by visitors to Atlanta to attend sporting events, conferences, conventions—or just to see the sights—the figure may just break your calculator. Try billions and billions.

This is no accident, of course. There is a group of folks—the Atlanta Convention and Visitors Bureau—who make it their job to sell Atlanta as a great place for corporate meetings, group meetings, and so on.

The leading facility for conventions is the Georgia World Congress, which is capable of meeting almost any group's

The Fox Theater has several meeting rooms

Even Stone Mountain (visible to the left) has a conference center

The Atlanta Apparel Mart

convention needs. And if the World Center cannot do it, then the Georgia Dome next door can. It can seat up to 70,000 people. Smaller audiences can overflow into the OMNI, which seats 16,000.

A lot of shows are held at the Atlanta Trade Center in the heart of Downtown. This is a cluster of several buildings—the Apparel Mart, the Gift Mart, the Merchandise Mart, and the Inforum. These marts have permanent displays that are open year around; they also produce a number of three-day shows which draw in buyers from all over.

Smaller facilities serve smaller meetings. The Fox Theater has two of the most elegant ballrooms or meeting rooms you could ever want. The Stone Mountain State Park has an executive resort which features access to all of its attractions—most notably the golf course. Hotels are all equipped to handle small meetings and groups as well.

The Democratic Party held its 1988 convention in Atlanta. In a sense, the Olympics will be like a grand-scale convention—for the best athletes in the world.

Of course, playing host to so many people requires more than just facilities and nerve. It requires a genuine sense of hospitality, a willingness on the part of all citizens of metro Atlanta to reach out and welcome the world.

Let's open our doors and hearts, and make the world feel at home.

On the floor at the Georgia World Congress convention center during a trade show

Atlanta Sports Trivia

Another trivia quiz, this time with an athletic twist. Lifelong residents are expected to know all the answers. Transplants are expected to know 80 percent. Visitors are given until 1996 to learn about Atlanta.

1. Atlanta Fulton County Stadium was originally built for use by which professional baseball team?

a. The Braves.
b. The Cherokees.
c. The Crackers.
d. The Peaches.

2. In what statistic did the Falcons lead the National Football League during 1992?

a. Net yardage.
b. Passing TDs.
c. First downs.
d. Most beer consumed in one game.

3. Which Atlanta professional team won a division title the first season in Atlanta?

a. The Braves.
b. The Falcons.
c. The Hawks.
d. The Knights.

4. What was the nickname of the major league hockey team that did not make it in Atlanta?

a. The Blades.
b. The Pucks.
c. The Flames.
d. The Bruisers.

5. What four titles did Bobby Jones win in 1927 for the Grand Slam in golf?

a. The Masters, the PGA, the U.S. Open, and the British Open.
b. The U.S. Amateur, the Scottish Open, the U.S. Open, and the Memorial.
c. The U.S. Amateur, the British Amateur, the U.S. Open, and the British Open.
d. The Masters, the PGA, the Open, and the Western.

6. Who was Atlanta's first female national tennis champion?

a. Bitsy Grant.
b. Babe Dedrickson.
c. Billy Jean King.
d. Becky Felton.

7. Who is the only Atlantan to head a U.S. entry into the America's Cup sailing competition?

a. Billy Payne.
b. Ted Turner.
c. Henry Grady.
d. Andrew Young.

11. Who is safe on second? a. Mark Lemke. b. Eddie Matthews. c. Ty Cobb. d. The Georgia Peach.

8. The most points ever scored against the Falcons in one game is:

a. 72, Miami, 1983.
b. 51, Lions, 1969.
c. 59, Rams, 1976.
d. 56, 49ers, 1992.

9. What Georgia college football team has most recently ended a season ranked No. 1?

a. Georgia Tech.
b. U. of Georgia.
c. Emory.
d. Morris Brown.

10. Where was Atlanta's first professional baseball park located?

a. Grant Park.
b. Piedmont Park.
c. Inman Park.
d. Georgia Tech.

ANSWERS:

1. C. The Atlanta Crackers played minor league ball until the arrival of the Braves. The last game they played was the first one in the new stadium.
2. B. 33 of them.
3. D, last year.
4. C.
5. C. Jones never played professionally.
6. A.
7. B.
8. C.
9. A. In 1990.
10. B.
11. C and D. The latter was his nickname.

Slam Dunked

The Hawks' season begins each fall in October and runs until March—or, it is always hoped, much later. Home games are played in the 16,000-seat Omni, which sits across from the World Congress Center at the end of International Boulevard, just a few blocks from Downtown.

As in the past few seasons, the key to the Hawk's success in 1993-94 will rest primarily in the hands of Dominique Wilkins and Kevin Willis. If they can stay healthy throughout the year and play up to their normal performance, the Hawks could well be a power to contend with.

With the retirement of Michael Jordan from the Bulls, Wilkins has an excellent shot at becoming the league's leading scorer. And the window of opportunity has been opened for the Hawks to fly in.

During the month of February 1992, the Hawks were the hottest team in the National Basketball Association, beating virtually every team they faced. When they managed to squeak into the playoffs—a contest that went down to the last games of the season—the outlook was promising. But April was not the same as February, and the Hawks were matched against the Chicago Bulls.

As well as the Hawks had played against the Bulls during the regular season, the post season is a different story. The Bulls stepped up their game a notch and swept the Hawks in four straight.

Can new head coach Lenny Wilkens restore the winning tradition to Atlanta? This is what the 1993-94 season will answer. Professional basketball is one of the most volatile of all sports. The acquisition of one key player—or coach—has been known to make an enormous difference.

Photos courtesy Atlanta Hawks

Law and Order

Civilization is a precarious thing. It is not just nature that mankind must conquer in order to live peacefully and successfully; it is his own inner nature as well. It was one thing to build railroads that connected Atlanta with the rest of the world, and buildings to live and work in; it was quite a different proposition to create a city of law and order.

In part because of the railroad, and in part because of the roughness of life in the mountains of Georgia, Atlanta has had something of a reputation for being a "fast town" ever since it began.

In 1847, just 10 years after the town was founded, the political wars in Atlanta were being fought not by Democrats and Republicans, but by the Rowdy Party versus the Moral Party. Four years later, a report stated that law and order in Atlanta was "perilously close to extinction."

When Atlanta fell to Sherman in 1864, the town suffered through several days of looting before the Union forces arrived to restore order. One hundred and thirty years later, it is easy to wonder if life has changed all that much, as the city still deals with the aftershocks of the rioting which followed the Rodney King verdicts in Los Angeles. In both instances, the citizens of the city took to the streets and destroyed their own neighborhoods.

After the war, the reputation continued. One part of Downtown, Whitehall Street (now Peters Street) from Decatur to Pryor was known as Snake Nation. Another desperate section of town was called Murrel's Row, in honor of John Murrel, a Tennessee outlaw.

Conditions did not improve with the turn of the century—in fact, with the emergence of the Ku Klux Klan, they seriously deteriorated. But, for all the terror they stirred up against blacks, Jews, and other minorities, they did serve one useful purpose. They flogged wife beaters. Without benefit of a trial, of course.

Some of the problems Atlanta has had to deal with were self-imposed, of course. Prohibition made moonshine illegal, thereby breeding a natural habitat for crime and racketeering. Once Prohibition was lifted, much of the crime vanished.

The same could be said for gambling rackets, which seemed to occupy a great deal of the attention of the local gendarmes. It has only been in the last year that Georgia made gambling legal by running a numbers game and a lottery itself. Had it been made legal 50, even 100 years ago, much of Atlanta's "crime" would not have been illegal.

At one point, operators of the bug games—the illegal gambling operations—were pardoned by Governor Eurith Rivers as quickly as they were arrested and convicted.

Even "legitimate" businesses found Atlanta a favorable town to operate in. Loan sharking was a big racket. The biggest shark of them all, Harold J. Smoot, charged as much as 240 percent annual interest on his loans.

As with any "fast town," Atlanta has had its share of prostitution—and still does. But what modern prostitute can compare with such legendary figures as Big Peck, a black prostitute who was reputed to be a lesbian; Big Millie, Black Rose, and Chilly Wind?

Is Atlanta still a "fast town?" To read the newspaper, it seems as if no real crime exists in the metro area. To watch TV news at 11 p.m., however, leaves a very much different impression. Hardly a day goes by that a child is not shot or stabbed at a school in Atlanta. But these are not the problems of a railroad town—they are problems every American city, and most foreign ones, are struggling with. On the whole Atlanta is doing well.

There will always be the spectacular murders, of course. The Sara Tokars slaying a year ago is no more typical of crime in the metro area than the highly publicized murders of days gone by. One was the murder of the son-in-law of Asa Candler, who was shot in a gun battle in his own home. The authorities responded to his wife's desperate phone call, but when they arrived could not tell who was who. They ended up shooting the dead man's son as well. He survived.

The papers love sensational murders of this kind—they sell papers. But they do not necessarily inform us about the safety of the streets. Atlanta has come a long, long way from 100 years ago, when highwaymen preyed regularly on folks traveling to and from Atlanta.

Hartsfield, after all, is as safe as any airport—and safer than most. The only crimes committed there are by good ole boys taking bribes.

Workin' on the Chain Gang

With crime, comes punishment. In many states, the punishment transpires entirely behind barred windows and walls. In Georgia, we still have our modern day version of the chain gang—prison work crews who are brought out into the community during the day to keep Georgia peachy clean by picking up trash along the highways, at airports, and in state parks, and working on other state and county projects.

You can usually spot one of these work crews; they are transported to the site in a corrections bus and work side by side, dressed in prison garb. These are run-of-the-mill offenders—no one who is a high security risk is assigned to outside work details. Still, 95 percent of the inmates at the county facilities make regular appearances working in the community.

The counties that benefit the most from this program are the ones that have allowed prison facilities to be built there. In many states, communities hate the thought of a prison—in the early days of Atlanta, it would have been called the "calaboose"—right next door to them. But in Georgia, we are able to see our tax dollars at work, doing things nobody really wants to do anyway.

The prospect of having to work on a prison chain gang may also have a deterring influence on crime. Not major crime, of course, such as murder. But shoplifting hardly seems worth the risk of being caught, thrown in the slammer, and then having to work in 100° weather picking up trash in July. It may not prevent the first offense, but it ought to be fairly powerful thereafter.

In addition to this program, the state also runs Georgia Correctional Industries, a public corporation which uses inmate labor to produce goods and services for state agencies and other tax-supported operations. During 1992, almost $17 million worth of goods and services were sold to the state and other agencies by GCI, while providing on-the-job training to inmates that will help them obtain and maintain jobs once released.

For whatever reason, the system seems to work. Georgia is one of the few states that can boast vacancies in its prison system. In fact, North Carolina recently asked Georgia to let it lease some of the empty space in Georgia's jails.

Whoever saw the possibility of making the Georgia prison system a profit center deserves to be memorialized. But while we are passing out praise, it also seems appropriate to suggest a few more areas in which prison labor could be put to work for the benefit of all Georgia:

- To pull down all the kudzu that is killing the pine trees along Georgia's highways.
- To have Japanese Zen monks teach our inmates how to transform raw kudzu into edible kudzu powder.
- To sell the powder to Japan, thereby eliminating this country's trade deficit.

All About Atlanta

As the Olympics approach, the focus of world wide media will zero in more and more on Atlanta. How well does the local media do in presenting a true image of the city—warts as well as beauty marks—to its residents?

There is certainly no shortage of media—and no drought of opinion, either. The newspaper scene is dominated by Cox Enterprises, which publishes both the morning *Constitution* and the afternoon *Journal*. As might be expected by a chain founded by a former Democratic candidate for President (James Cox of Ohio, who lost to Warren Harding of Ohio in 1920), these papers present the news through a liberal focus. This perspective plays very well in the city of Atlanta, but tends to drive readers living outside the Perimeter up the wall.

The best thing about the *Constitution* is Lewis Grizzard, a columnist who is reprinted in many papers nationwide but who actually lives and works here. He became the news himself in 1993, when he almost died on the operating table. But his heart is fixed now, and Lewis is back.

Marietta has its own daily paper, the *Daily Journal,* but they are not big enough to represent an alternative, except in their limited area. The same is true about the *Atlanta Daily World*, a black-owned daily newspaper which enjoys strong support in the black community, but does not make much of an impact beyond it.

For a short while, the *New York Times* tried to compete with the Cox empire through the *Daily News,* headquartered in Gwinnett County. But that did not add all that much true diversity to the reporting of the news, and Cox beat them to a pulp with an advertising rate war.

A fresh upstart, printed weekly, is *Creative Loafing,* which covers the entertainment scene but also ventures into political coverage from time to time. A new spinoff for the folks north of the Perimeter is *Topside Loaf,* which just made its appearance.

There are a number of magazines that deal with the Atlanta area. The most established is *Atlanta*—but it was owned by American Express until recently, when it was sold. *Atlanta Homes and Lifestyles* is likewise owned by extra-Atlantan interests; it is primarily oriented toward covering the latest styles in decorating and remodeling homes in the metro area.

Peachtree, on the other hand, bills itself as "the guide to the civilized South," and deals with just about any subject that fits that description—especially if it is expensive.

Like any big city, Atlanta has a whole gaggle of radio stations, each carving out its own comfortable niche. There is a classical music radio station, any number of rock stations, even more country stations, and a growing number of talk stations.

Kudzu's somewhat eclectic radio tastes run from Randy and Spiff in the morning to Rush Limbaugh in the afternoon, and the Braves at night, when they are playing, with classical music at random, when it is playing.

Television is represented by local affiliates of each of the Big 3 networks; plus Fox, PBS, and WTBS; plus a couple of independent stations (Channels 46 and 69). The news programming is pretty much indistinguishable from one station to the next, except on Channel 46, which airs an hour long news show at 10 p.m. On the whole, there is way too much reporting of car wrecks and rapes, and not enough on the issues and people that make Atlanta what it is.

Mystery Tonight?

The most delightful high-crime zone in Atlanta is Agatha's Mystery Theater, located at 673 Peachtree Street in Midtown. At least one murder occurs on stage every night of the week, usually between hors d'oeuvre and soup. But the mystery is always cleared up by dessert, all without the help of the local constabulary.

Instead, it is the audience that is called on to solve the crime. For Agatha's specializes in participatory theater, and they structure the action around dinner. Patrons assemble by 7:30 (7 on Sundays) to indulge in a five-course dinner and to play their parts in the scheduled hijinks.

As each person arrives (advance reservations are an absolute must), he or she is assigned a character to play—or a song to sing.

As the audience digests their assignments—and wait for the rest of the crowd to gather—they are invited to help themselves to hors d'oeurves, which might range from mini egg rolls to antipasto to shrimp dainties. The appetizers are all scrumptious and tend to disappear rapidly.

When the crowd has assembled, the action begins. Using just two or three actors, each playing several roles, the plot unfolds—or, if you prefer, unravels. In a recent production, "The Curse of Dead Dude Ranch," General Colon Bowel is killed by the Teddy Bear Slasher, a.k.a. the King of the Teddy Bears. The action is a loose send-up of the Billy Crystal movie *City Slickers.* Almost like stepping into the *Twilight Zone,* the audience becomes campers at a Western dude ranch, led by trail boss Billy Pistol.

A guest gets a new identity

Audience members have all been given new identities, to fit the character they portray—Newt Goodwrench, Sam None, Wyatt Burp, and others. The plot helps set the pretense, but is not terribly important—the fun comes from watching other members of the audience take their turn at becoming stars, as well as enjoying the professional actors ham it up.

The plays are all written in-house—most of them by Tom Williams, who also is part of the cast. Each play runs about 10 weeks and then changes, for a total of five different plays a year. The audience is asked to dress casually or in outfits that suit the nature of the play.

Each act lasts about 20 minutes, followed by another course of dinner. Unlike many dinner theaters, at Agatha's the food is every bit as delectable as the action. There are meat, fish, chicken, and vegetarian entrées.

Upcoming plays will be "The Case of the Misguided Mistletoe," "Dying with Oscar," and "Cat on a Hot Tin Streetcar."

Agatha's Mystery Theater provides a singular theater experience. It's great fun.

Tickets cost $33 to $38 and include the show, dinner, and wine. Reservations can be made by calling 875-1610.

The Coach and Six

Back in the days before Henry Ford made it possible for all of us to have a least one car in the garage, a reliable sign of one's stature in the community was the size of his livery. A man on foot had nothing to boast about. A man on a horse fared a good deal better. Add a carriage and your reputation rose rapidly.

The epitome of luxury was to have "a coach and six," meaning a carriage that was drawn by six horses, plus all the stablehands and attendants that would be required to maintain such equipage.

The Coach and Six, a restaurant on Peachtree between Midtown and Buckhead, strives to recreate the elegant luxury that anyone who could have afforded a coach and six would have expected. And they do admirably well.

The emphasis is placed equally on creating a relaxed, inviting ambiance, producing wonderful food in the classic tradition, and serving it with grace and style.

The atmosphere is dark and quiet; the intent is to suggest the mood of an English club. The effect is heightened by elaborate sideboards and rich paintings.

The food is better than you might expect in most English clubs, and not as hidebound in tradition. We started with a black bean soup, for which the Coach and Six is justly famous. Served with rice and onions on the side, it is a remarkable work of culinary art.

Also first-rate was the tomato and buffalo mozzarella salad, which is served with greens and a basil dressing. But be warned: the salad is really too large to serve as a dinner salad. Two can split it quite nicely.

For the main course, we had the filet mignon with bearnaise and veal oscar. The filet was a gorgeous piece of meat, broiled to order. It can be ordered with a green peppercorn sauce as well as the bearnaise.

The veal Oscar was topped with Dungeness crabmeat instead of the standard Alaskan, and was finished off expertly with fresh asparagus and bearnaise—a very enjoyable dish, indeed.

Other entrées that tempted us included triple cut lamb chops, roasted Georgia quail, and cinnamon roasted duck. Each entrée is served with complementary accompaniments, but aspargus, spinach, mushrooms, and potatoes can also be ordered as additional sides.

For dessert, the waiter rolls a multi-layered cart of all kinds of cakes, tortes, and other sweet things up to the table. We tried a chocolate mousse torte that was a wonderful conclusion to the meal, then sipped on cappucino.

At every stage of the meal, the service was alert and responsive.

The Coach and Six has an extensive wine cellar with one of the largest bottles of champagne we have ever seen. The cost to purchase the bottle: somewhere in the vicinity of $900. Bring lots of friends.

Although expensive, the Coach and Six is a great place for any celebration. For reservations, call 872-6666. It is located at 1776 Peachtree Road.

Jimmy Carter Library

A dog cools off by the Japanese garden

Each president of the United States tries to leave a legacy, to inspire future generations. For Jimmy Carter, the only citizen of Georgia to serve as President, this legacy is still taking shape—in the form of the Jimmy Carter Library and Carter Presidential Center in Virginia Highlands, just off Highland at 1 Copenhill.

Situated on a high knoll with a majestic view of Downtown, the library and surrounding grounds are open to the public daily. The library is not a library as much as it is a museum chronicling the highlights of the Carter presidency, complete with a full scale replica of the Oval Office, a display of inaugural gowns worn by first ladies, personal mementoes, and much more. The grounds include a lovely Japanese garden.

The Carter Center is not open to the public, but is the nerve center for what Carter wants to become "a great resource." A first step in the unfolding of that dream has been the initiation of the Atlanta Project, a bold attempt to restore prosperity and hope to the poorer sections of Atlanta—with the idea of making Atlanta a model for what cities can become.

The Wren's Nest

At the turn of the century, he was one of the most famous American authors alive. He was admired by President Theodore Roosevelt. He was a friend of Mark Twain. He was called on by Philanthropist Andrew Carnegie when he came to Atlanta to dedicate its new public library. His Uncle Remus stories were translated into other languages and published throughout the world.

By the 1950's, however, he was being discredited, even in the city he called home. He was charged with being a racist and perpetuating racial stereotypes—obviously by people who had never read his stories.

Now, 100 years after his emergence as an important American writer, Joel Chandler Harris is once again being recognized for the contributions he made—a unique writer who preserved a rich treasure of Afro-American folk stories and made them available to the American public.

String Man helped Harris handle rowdy kids

The best monument to his talent as the creator of Uncle Remus is the Wren's Nest, the home he lived in on Ralph David Abernathy Boulevard in the West End. When Harris first moved his wife and nine children to this home, he was just a reporter on the Atlanta *Constitution,* working for the legendary Henry Grady.

It was a small home then, but a couple of renovations transformed it into a magical Victorian masterpiece, full of fancy and imagination. It was largely in its final shape by the time he became editor of the *Constitution*—and started to attract national notice through his stories.

He eventually retired from the *Constitution* to work full time on his stories, but he returned to active journalism to edit a national magazine called the *Uncle Remus Home Journal.*

The Wren's Nest acquired its name after a family of wrens tooks up residence in the Harris mailbox. Folks started giving directions "to the sign of the wren's nest," and the appellation stuck.

Many homes of famous people are fairly dull stops on the obligatory tour of any city. But the Wren's Nest is a delightful exception to this tendency. For one thing, it is a marvelous example of how the middle class lived at the turn of the century. The last room added by Harris, for instance, was an indoor bathroom; he believed that it was unsanitary to bring the bathroom indoors.

For another, the group that keeps the house open also keeps it lively. They sponsor almost continual storytelling sessions each day from 10 to 2. The stories are taken from the nine volumes of Uncle Remus stories, but updated for contemporary audiences. Call 753-7735 for information.

Be sure to roost a while at the Wren's Nest.

UNCLE REMUS'S
JANUARY 1909
PRICE TEN CENTS
Founded By JOEL CHANDLER HARRIS

The Best in the World

In 1911, Bill Hartsfield rode out to a racetrack owned by Asa Candler in Hapeville to watch an acrobatic aerial competition of aircraft—just eight years after the Wright brothers proved the possibility of flight at Kitty Hawk. He was fascinated with what he saw there—and remained fascinated with it for the rest of his life.

Which was good for Atlanta, because Hartsfield, who eventually became mayor of Atlanta, became one of the driving forces behind the establishment and expansion of Atlanta as a major international airport.

Today, the airport that bears Hartsfield's name is the largest single-site employer in Georgia, employing 40,000 people. More than 40 million people fly in and out of Hartsfield each year. On the average, 1,700 flights a day take off and land at the facility.

It would have been hard for Hartsfield to imagine what the little stretch of land he was standing on in 1911 would become. Even when Charles Lindbergh visited Atlanta in 1927, following his transoceanic flight, the airport consisted of two hangars and two dirt landing strips—no terminal or even office for the manager.

It was air mail and crop dusting that enabled Atlanta to emerge into a major airport facility. Gradually, as more people began to fly—especially to Florida from northern climes—Atlanta became a hub for passenger travel, too.

The new international concourse is nearing completion

Just how important is Hartsfield to Atlanta? In 1991, the airport ranked as fourth largest in the world in aircraft operations and sixth in the world in passengers served. Only Chicago, Dallas-Fort Worth, and Los Angeles are larger in the United States.

The airport suffered a momentary shock with the collapse of Eastern Air Lines, which had occupied the entire C Concourse. The concourse was shut down for awhile, but has now been reopened in part as TWA expands its service in and out of Atlanta.

Actually, the airport is almost always expanding—or at least evolving. Construction is nearing completion on a new international concourse, a $300 million project which should be completed by spring of 1994.

At the same time, work has begun on remodeling the terminal. When the sawdust stops flying, life at the terminal will revolve around a "town center" of shops and food services that will soar sky high to a glass-domed atrium. This project should be completed by November of 1994, giving Hartsfield an entirely new feel inside.

In truth, however, most of the airport's functions are never seen by most travelers. The average traveler becomes acquainted with the ticket counter, the metal detectors, the robotic trains, the gate areas, and perhaps baggage claim. But far from the terminal are other parts of the airport—most notably, a huge cargo center which handles 650,000 metric tons of cargo each year. Nine of the airlines that fly in and out of Atlanta on a daily basis carry only cargo—they have no passengers.

Atlanta has come a long way since that fall day in 1911. But without Hartsfield's vision and determination, it is unlikely that Atlanta would have the premier airport it is so proud to boast of today—an airport that has been acclaimed by frequent flyers as "the best in the world."

Passing through security

At the baggage carousel

The First Gold Rush

The town square in Dahlonega

Built as a courthouse; now a museum

Panning for gold at Crisson's Mine

In Cherokee, the word for "gold" is "Tahlonega." When the first white man heard the word, he did not wait around long enough to get the pronunciation correct. He picked up his shovel and headed for Dahlonega, the site of the first big gold rush in the United States—20 years before Sutter's Creek, 70 years before Alaska. And, if the truth be known, there is still gold in dem dar hills—the mountains of north Georgia, that is.

How much gold was mined out of Dahlonega? Enough to warrant building a U.S. Mint in the heart of downtown. Enough to make the mint one of the first properties seized by the Confederate Army during the Civil War. Enough to make Dahlonega a genuine boom town until all the fever settled down—or more precisely, spread elsewhere.

A massive crusher sits idle, a memory of times past

Dahlonega is now a charming tourist center. The town center is surrounded by enough shops to keep you busy for an afternoon; the old mint has been converted to a museum on gold and Dahlonega.

Of course, it was gold that brought the prospectors to Dahlonega, and so any visit to the area should include a stop at one of the local mines, such as Crisson's Gold Mine on Wimpy Mill Road, where you can learn to pan for gold—and perhaps even come out ahead. Serious panners come back many times a season, in hopes of finding enough tiny specks to add up to something worthwhile.

In addition to the panning, Crisson's still has the heavy machinery they used to crush the rock that was extracted from the mine, thereby liberating the gold.

Crisson's is open every day. In addition to the panning, they have a gift shop with jewelry and souvenirs.

Hobbit Hall

It is never too early to encourage the habit of reading in children; it feeds their natural curiosity. If children are read to, they will take it upon themselves to learn to read, and develop a habit that can serve them well for their entire life.

Hobbit Hall is a charming bookstore in Roswell that is dedicated to the proposition that the world of childhood is best explored through books.

Situated in a white cottage just down the street from historic Bulloch Hall, the store is like something out of a fairy tale—a neat, tidy house on the outside that seems to be a never-ending castle of books, puzzles, and neat things to do on the inside.

This is one store that decidedly encourages browsing. And once you have bought your selection, there are plenty of decks and patios where you can sit and read what you have just bought— if your child cannot wait until you get home!

Hobbit Hall is exceptionally well stocked; the range of books on mythology alone is impressive. One entire room is dedicated to books on science (for older kids); another side room is filled with books for the nursery and toddlers.

The proprietors obviously know what they are doing, showing a discerning taste in their choice of books to stock and promote.

They also regularly hold author signings for the better-known authors in the children's field.

Whether you are shopping for everyday reading for your own kids, or are looking for birthday or Christmas gifts for youngsters, the Hobbit Hall should be your first stop.

Hobbit Hall is located a half block west of Roswell Mill, on the south side of Bulloch Lane. It can also be reached off of Roswell Road to Marietta.

If you want to help a child sharpen his or her curiosity, this is the place to come.

A Peach of a Place To Meet

Lunch is served on the Terrace; golf is just minutes away at Brae Linn Country Club

For years, when a business would hold a meeting, they would schedule it at a local hotel. Tables and chairs would be set up in a big square, and everyone would sit there for a day or two, getting sore rear ends.

It is good news that alternatives are beginning to appear—and one of them is in Peachtree City, just south of Atlanta. Called The Peachtree Executive Conference Center, it is a compound devoted exclusively to helping businesses stage meetings.

The center consists of 33 meeting rooms with capacities from 12 to 600, a 250-room hotel for out-of-town guests, two restaurants, a golf course, swimming pool, a variety of indoor sports, a workout room, and a "Team Challenge" course.

The meeting rooms are all state-of-the-art in terms of audio-visual equipment and other meeting or training aids. Chairs are designed for all-day marathon seating—and the recreational facilities make it easy to unwind.

The facility has become popular with corporate training programs throughout the country; a single unit may send 20 to 100 people to Peachtree for a week or two of training in new technical skills.

On weekends, when businesses are not apt to be holding meetings, rooms can be booked without attending a meeting. It can be a great getaway. For information, call (404) 487-2000.

Rooms are available to seat anywhere from 12 to 600 people in state-of-the-art comfort

Checquers

It is odd that when people list their favorite restaurants, they inevitably include at least one expensive steak house—and just as inevitably overlook seafood restaurants.

This may have something to do with Catholics being forced to eat too many fish sticks on too many Fridays—or with the simple fact that until recently, it was difficult to ship fish to an inland city like Atlanta and keep it fresh.

Both of these problems have been solved now, the first by the Pope and the second by the air cargo industry. So it is time to revise our prejudices and our presumptions and recognize that some of the very finest restaurants in metro Atlanta specialize in seafood.

We have always had outstanding meals at the Savannah Fish Co. (in the Westin Peachtree hotel downtown) and at L & N Seafood across Ashford-Dunwoody from the Perimeter Mall, just northeast of the intersection of Georgia 400 and I-285.

But probably the best—and most popular—of all is Checquers, located right around the corner from L & N on Hammond Drive.

Everything about Checquers is impressive. Its tables are laid out so that no diners feel as though they are on top of the next party. In fact, parties of six or eight are seated in semi-private rooms, so that there is no constant reshuffling of tables and chairs to accommodate such groups.

The decor is of the sea, but not offensively so. In some seafood restaurants, it is possible to contract *mal de mer* just looking at the harpoons and netting hanging on the wall. At Chequers, the sea is evoked more subtly, primarily through artwork.

But the great achievement of Checquers is, of course, the food. Everything we sampled was excellent. We started with a bowl of clam chowder and a sliced tomato and red onion salad. The clam chowder was served New England style and was first-rate. The tomatoes were ripe (why is this a surprise?) and topped with bleu cheese. It was excellent.

For dinner, we selected the baked flounder and fresh grouper grilled over mesquite. A baked dish is often the downfall of seafood restaurants, because it is so easy to overcook the fish. Fresh can become dry and tasteless in a hurry in the oven. But the flounder was still moist and delicate. Each filet had been wrapped around a stuffing of shrimp and scallops, then covered with a mornay sauce. The result was a huge success.

So was the grilled grouper, which melted in the mouth. But as delicious as the grouper was, it was almost secondary to the mashed potatoes that came with it. These potatoes had been mashed with roasted garlic and topped with natural gravy. Here's hoping they never replace this side item on the menu.

The same can be said about the sweet drop biscuits which are served hot throughout the meal. Wonderful!

For dessert, we sampled their key lime pie. Key lime pies can be pretty bland at times, but this one had a zing that woke up your taste buds once again. It was a great ending to a superior meal.

When it comes right down to it, there are a lot more interesting things a chef can do with fish than with a steak. Any number of items on the Checquers' menu tempt us to come back, like the lure of the Sirens to Odysseus. The fresh grilled tuna topped with a shrimp salsa sounds divine, as do the jumbo Maryland-style crabcakes.

As one of our Kudzu undercover team remarked as we left Checquers, "If seafood always tasted this good, I might not eat anything else."

And she loves steak.

Who Does Give A Damn?

When we first created our nominee for alternate mascot of Atlanta, Whogivesadamn, we thought of him as a cute, slightly irreverent satire. But the more we investigated the pluses and minuses of the city for this book, the more we began to realize that he might not be a satire after all. Instead of Atlanta's alternate mascot, he may actually be the city's alter ego.

We hope not, because we believe that Atlanta has a tremendous potential—a potential that embraces far more than the Super Bowl this year and the Olympics in 1996.

We wanted to tap this potential, and set aside this space at the end of the book for interviews with prominent makers and shakers of metro Atlanta.

We contacted a dozen of them—all very well-known names. We thought they would be delighted to be interviewed about their vision for Atlanta, and how to implement it. We asked Democrats and Republicans; elected officials and sacred legends; black and white; men and women.

Not one agreed to be interviewed.

This disturbed us, because everyone we asked is a fine person, a proven leader. But no one would step forward and speak for Atlanta.

In desperation, with two empty pages glaring at us from the galley proofs, we turned to Whogivesadamn and asked him to comment on his vision of Atlanta. This is what he said:

"No one has ever given a great speech in Atlanta. They go to New York or Washington or somewhere else, where they know people listen to speeches. Atlanta is not a town where people listen to speeches. It is not because they do not give a damn. It is because they are so busy following their own vision, their own dream.

"So don't worry that no one wanted to be interviewed. They are too busy already, each of them trying to make Atlanta great.

"Most of the beautiful, exciting, and wonderful things that you have written about in this book came about because someone got busy and followed their dream. Sometimes it was a single person acting alone—Art Rilling creating the Yellow River Game Ranch or Alonzo Herndon showing the whole world that blacks can succeed; they can live in the expensive house on top of the hill. In other cases, it was a group of people—often a not-for-profit group that had to go out and solicit funds to make their slice of the dream come to pass. In a few cases, it is government that helped the dream become a reality.

"These folks did not wait for a master plan to be handed down to them from above. They went out and created as they saw fit. And the result is what we view as special and wonderful here in Atlanta.

"Atlanta is not a city of dreamers; it is a city that has been built by people who were not afraid to act on their dreams—build on their dreams. This is why Atlanta has become so much so fast. It takes people who know how to get things done to build a city like this.

"And the great thing is that they are not done. Atlanta has not reached its peak, ready to decline. This may be true of some neighborhoods, but they can be restored. It just takes someone with a dream.

"For its part, the community needs to see the truth in this. There are enough visionaries to keep this city hopping for decades to come. What Atlanta needs are doers—people who are able to put their dreams to work."

Having said that, the little fellow went off and chugged a can of beer, leaving us with our thoughts. We began to understand what he was trying to say—that there is a dynamic spirit that is alive and well in Atlanta and pushing the city in the right direction.

As we visited each of the attractions in this book, we were amazed at how many of them have relied on the support of the community to do what they have done—and have gotten it. They have gone out, asked for funding, found it, and have built something wonderful with it. Now the community reaps the rewards of its own generosity.

Look at some of the many institutions that developed in this way:

- The Fox Theater, which was saved from the wreckers ball, only to become a showplace of the arts.
- The Center for Puppetry Arts, which has developed a remarkable program.
- Fernbank Museum of Natural History, which is a colossal achievement.
- The Atlanta History Center.

• The Chattahoochee Nature Center.

Take away community support and what do you have left? Nothing.

This point was demonstrated to us poignantly during our visit to the Chattahoochee Nature Center, a nonprofit group that almost went under a few years ago but reorganized and is now stronger than ever.

During the heavy snowfall Atlanta experienced last April, part of the protective netting for the aviary was torn down. The naturalists were able to rescue the birds before they flew away in confusion, but were unable to fix it themselves. While we were touring the premises, however, a number of Georgia Power cherry pickers pulled up and went to work placing new posts and stringing new meshing, all as a donation.

Across the road, we also saw where the boardwalk trail into the swamp along the river had been damaged and needed replacing. We then saw a pile of planks—and a lot of finished boardwalk where volunteers had come in and handled the carpentry.

This is a remarkable story—an achievement that the whole community should take pride in. It is the basis for President Carter's proposed Atlanta Project—and it will work, so long as it does not get managed to death. If something that will be good for the community needs to be done, the people of Atlanta will find a way to get it done.

If they are left out of the process, they may seem indifferent, even hostile. Whogivesadamn seems to be the appropriate message. But if they are advised of the need, they will find a way to meet it.

This is the glory and the hope for Atlanta. It is a tradition that has been building for 140 years, and it can continue to lead us into the next century. It is a tradition each of us must guard in our hearts, and expand through our lives.

Through your actions, you can make Whogivesadamn a local hero—not as an expression of indifference and nonchalance, but as an expression of commitment and interest.

If we work together as a community, we can demonstrate what can be done when people support the best and noblest activities around them.

The best and noblest that Atlanta can produce is still in the future. We are the ones who must seize the dream and make it real.

How To Get Yours

If you have enjoyed reading *The Super Unofficial Atlanta Souvenir Guide,* we would like to sell you some more copies. Give it to friends here in Atlanta who never get out and do anything. Give it to friends who are planning to visit Atlanta from overseas. If you are just visiting, send copies to friends back home, as the ultimate way to say: "Wish you were here."

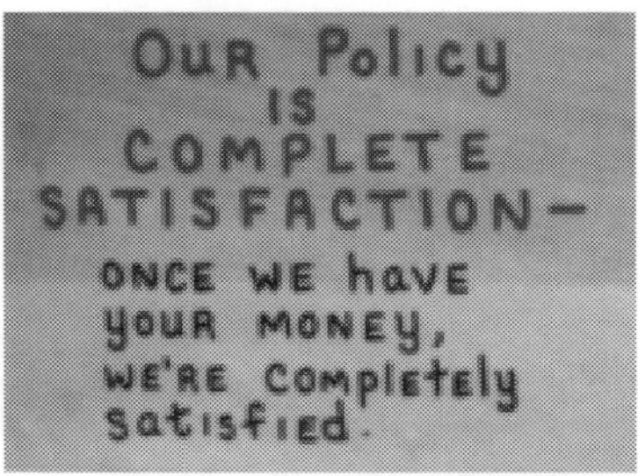

Sign in Dahlonega store

Single copies of the book can be purchased for $17.95 plus 5.5 percent for the state of Georgia. Enclose $2 for shipping.

Five or more copies can be bought for $15 each, plus sales tax and $5 for shipping.

Ten or more copies can be bought for $12 apiece, plus sales tax and $8 for shipping.

We also have Whogivesadamn T-shirts for sale at $19.95 apiece, plus 5.5 percent sales tax and $2 for shipping.

If a T-shirt is bought at the same time as a book, the combined price is just $30, plus 5.5 percent sales tax and $3 for shipping.

A significant donation to charity is made for every T-shirt sold.

If you want to become a member of the Whogivesadamn fan club, we can help you there, too. For dues of $35, you will receive a free Whogivesadamn T-shirt, a certificate of membership, reports on the tireless efforts of Whogivesadamn to serve as alternate mascot, and 10 percent off any other Whogivesadamn merchandise.

To order, send a check or money order for the proper amount to Enthea Press, P.O. Box 1387, Alpharetta, GA 30239-1387. Or call us at locally at 664-4886 or toll free at 1-800-336-7769 and place your order by phone. We accept VISA, American Express, and MasterCard.